Contents

■

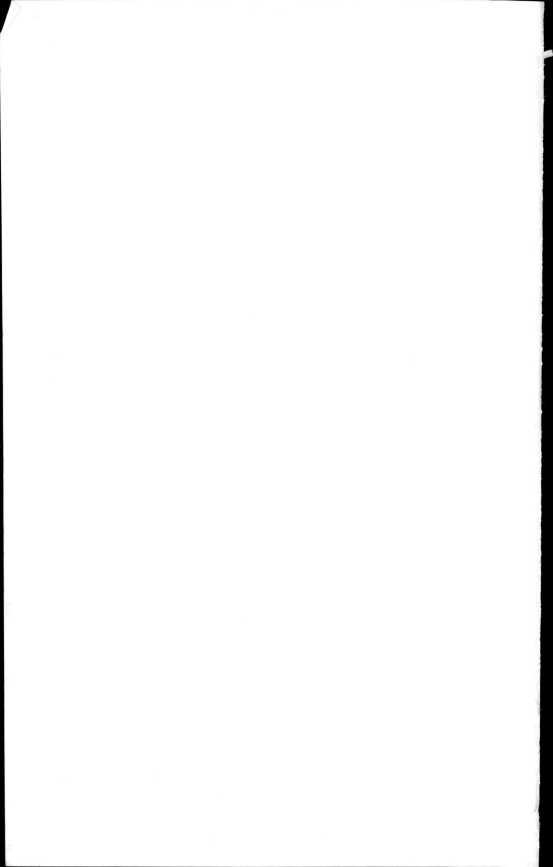

Achieving Environmental Management Standards

A Step-by-step Guide to BS7750

■

MICHAEL J. GILBERT

The Institute of Management (IM) is at the forefront of management development and best management practice. The Institute embraces all levels of management from students to chief executives. It provides a unique portfolio of services for all managers, enabling them to develop skills and achieve management excellence. If you would like to hear more about the benefits of membership, please write to Department P, Institute of Management, Cottingham Road, Corby NN17 1TT.
This series is commissioned by the Institute of Management Foundation.

The publisher's policy is to use **paper manufactured from sustainable forests**

Pitman Publishing
128 Long Acre, London WC2E 9AN

A Division of Longman Group UK Limited

First published in 1993

Reprinted 1993

A CIP catalogue record for this book can be obtained from the British Library

ISBN 0 273 60079 6

Photoset in Linotron Century Schoolbook by
Northern Phototypesetting Co., Ltd., Bolton
Printed by Bell and Bain Ltd., Glasgow

Preface

■

The design of this handbook came from discussions with the British Institute of Management and Pitman Publishing following publication of the draft proposals for a European-wide environmental audit scheme (the Eco-audit Regulation) and BS7750: Specification for environmental management systems in 1992. The proposed Regulation, subsequently changed to the Eco-management and audit Regulation and British Standard provide fresh impetus for industry managers to re-think how they can improve their organisations' environmental performance; and through that improvement, make a contribution to the business and community effort to achieve the sustainable development goal. Both documents provide the opportunity to improve business activities through the involvement and motivation of managers and staff, allowing business leaders to reach out and touch all those whose activities have an impact on the environment. Both documents focus on the need for organisations to integrate environmental management into day-to-day operations and both establish standards of environmental management system design and performance. Both documents encourage a proactive approach to environmental improvement through analysing the environmental effects of the organisation, establishing environmental policies, setting objectives and targets for performance improvement, establishing an improvement programme, and an audit system to track and report environmental management system performance against requirements.

The regulation includes requirements for member states' activities in support of the scheme, the role, qualifications and protocols related to the verification, public statement criteria on environmental performance and participation as well as criteria for environmental management systems and audits.

BS7750 was designed to meet the management system standardisation needs of the proposed Regulation with the exception of the public statement requirement, and, as the Standard is a published document, and the Regulation has yet to come into force, this handbook will focus on BS7750. Later editions will be updated to reflect the final regulation contents. This approach will provide management with a tool to address environmental management problems today, confident that they can meet developing European standards and legislation.

Many guides have been written about the content and intent of the proposed regulation and BS7750. Even more has been written on the concept of 'environmental auditing' and the requirements of internal environmental protection systems or environmental management systems. However, at workshops and conferences where the background and concept of BS7750 is explained the most usual response from managers is, 'We understand *what* is required, but *how* do we go about getting there?'

What seems to be required therefore is a handbook that shows, through a practical approach, how to establish an environmental management system to meet the requirements of the Standard and the proposed Regulation. To be really useful then, this book is not just an explanation of the requirements of effective environmental management systems (although that forms a part of the book); rather, it is designed to provide guidance on an approach. It treats the implementation of environmental management systems as a project activity, with suggestions on objectives and methods, examples, communication hints and tips. In it you will find steps for a project manager to meet a particular objective: an environmental management system that meets the requirements of BS7750, that is integrated into the management system of your own organisation.

If, in the light of your own experiences, you feel some improvement could be made, please write to the publisher so that future revisions will include positive proposals for changes and improvements.

Project management is not about luck, so I include no good luck message! However, whenever you think it is getting difficult, ponder the words of Carlyle: '*Every noble work is at first impossible*'.

Mike Gilbert
February 1993

1

Introduction

Applying the concept of sustainable development is difficult!

It sets new environmental performance requirements for society and industry that bring change in many ways, from the domestic use of bottle banks to national decisions on policy and investment. Environmental requirements for industry arise as pressures from outside or as opportunities to achieve benefits from inside. Whether a large company or a small company, the opportunities and potential benefits are great and the risks of non-compliance equally high.

Yet the practice of meeting performance requirements is not a new one for managers, as they strive to meet customer requirements all the time. To help them meet these requirements, industry uses quality system standards as tools to establish appropriate practices and procedures to assure success, the quality management standards, BS5750, act as a benchmark for industry.

In meeting the new environmental performance requirements, whether for products or organisations, industry needs new benchmarks to demonstrate their progress, through an **environmental management systems** approach.

These models of good environmental management can be applied by any organisation, and like the quality systems approach, assured success in this area is becoming an important consideration in the business development plans of many organisations, supporting the progress towards the sustainable development goal.

The concept of sustainable development

The concept of sustainable development, defined by the World Commission on Environment and Development, has become accepted by politicians and industry leaders as a guiding philosophy. It ensures that the use of environmental resources to meet current needs is managed so as not to damage those resources for future use.

> This means living on the earth's income rather than eroding its capital. It means keeping the consumption of renewable resources within the limits of their replenishment. It means handing down to successive generations not only man-made wealth (such as buildings, roads and railways) but also natural wealth, such as clean and adequate water supplies, good arable land, a wealth of wildlife and ample forests. (*This Common Inheritance*, HMSO)

The principles of sustainable development involve the process of integrating environmental criteria into economic practice to ensure that the strategic plans of organisations, while satisfying the need for continuing growth and evolution, conserve nature's 'capital' for the future. Applying the principle implies living within the carrying capacity of existing eco-systems. This will require a change in many aspects of society and commerce. It is not only about air pollution, ozone depletion, water conservation, raw material use and waste management; it is also a truly international issue, affecting cross-border transactions, trade, finance and political agendas.

The role of industries which operate on an international basis is therefore key to a constructive approach to achieve the sustainable development goal. Industry influences the source of raw materials, the manufacturing and distribution processes, the consumers' responses and the methods of waste disposal through their activities. A proactive lead from industry to find positive incentives to change and improve environmental performance would mean opportunities for less legislative control, a healthier communication process with the community and ultimately a sustainable industrial and social future for us all. This is where defined standards of environmental management conformity can help.

The quality concept has led to a revolution in many organisations to transform themselves to meet the need to assure customers of their organisation's internal quality management system capacity to produce products and services that meet the purchasers specified requirements. As a result many organisations seek certification to defined, international, quality system standards – ISO9000. An assessed and certified quality system capability provides a 'badge' that signifies an attained level. Quality assured status is now a growing requirement across all sectors of commerce in the UK.

Imagine, then, an international standard that provides a vehicle for assured **environmental** management system performance. Although not a solution to sustainable development, the existence of an environmental management system along the lines of BS7750 provides for the integration of environmental criteria into an organisation's performance criteria at all levels. A supporting certification scheme could provide external visibility and assurance of the organisation's commitment and performance, providing market differentiation for those who meet the criteria and a 'badge' as an incentive or reward for those willing to meet the requirements. Being a voluntary scheme, it would provide industry with a self-regulatory basis for continual improvement in environmental performance through the audit and review process.

Environmental management performance

Organisations today are under many pressures to manage and improve their environmental performance: to comply with more stringent legislation and to satisfy customer demands. The drivers are powerful and diverse, and, in spite of a severe recession, do not appear to be receding.

Legislation demands improved performance through the Environmental Protection Act (EPA) and enabling legislation like the Integrated Pollution Control (IPC) Act and Waste Liability Directives. Other legislation is planned, both in the UK and in Europe which will include regulations on packaging, product labelling and eco-auditing. The new legislation will follow the principle of 'the polluter pays'. This will increase the pressure on companies to ensure that their pollution levels are known and managed to the lowest possible levels. For example, in a recent case a small oil tank on a temporary site was vandalised. As a result diesel oil leaked into a local stream. The company that owned the tank was not only fined for the breach of consent, but it also had to bear the cost of all the cleaning up, including soil removal and disposal, which exceeded the fine.

Duty of Care regulations and strict liability laws mean that breaches of discharge consents or failure to control waste materials can have significant financial penalties that far outweigh the direct costs of a system failure. These can include withdrawal of consent and business closure.

Best environmental options (BEO), Best available techniques not exceeding excessive cost (BATNEEC) and environmental impact assessments (IEA) are beginning to place the legislators' interests into the company decision-making processes. Consumers, and this includes purchasers in the supply chain, are exerting pressure on companies to provide more environmentally appropriate choices. For example, without prescriptive legislation, the use of CFCs as a propellant in domestic products almost disappeared in a two-year period as a direct result of pressure from consumers and pressure groups. Major companies like IBM, Boots and B&Q are questioning not just the environmental performance of the products they purchase, but also that of the organisation which makes the product.

Banks, insurance companies and shareholders exert pressure. National Westminster Bank requires an environmental impact assessment before releasing funds on certain loans. Insurance companies require higher premiums for companies with poor environmental performance records and will not insure some environmental risks because of the extensive liabilities incurred. Shareholders now have options to join 'Green Funds' where the investment criteria include the commitment to environmental 'clean technologies', waste minimisation or other aspects of good environmental performance.

A recent study by the Loss Prevention Council, 'Pollutant Industries' Report SHE 8:1992 identified twenty-five high-risk industries and their pollutants. In particular, it focused on six: agriculture; food; metal processing; paint; tanning; and textiles. The report provides some considered conclusions for insurers and reviews the implications for risk assessment.

Peer pressure can also be a significant factor. The concept of sustainable development is now embraced by many business and government leaders. It means that current operating activities should meet the needs of present stakeholders (shareholders, employees, customers and communities) without compromising the ability of future generations to meet their needs.

The drivers which 'cost' organisations environmentally, whether through loss of business, large fines, higher insurance premiums or negative publicity, are called 'negative' motivators. However, there is a positive side to improving environmental performance – the 'positive' motivators.

The concepts of reduction, reuse and recycling are not just slogans thought up by environmentalists. Application of such concepts can bring real cash savings to any organisation. Reduction of energy consumption and waste within an organisation saves money. Many companies have tried (and failed) to run energy management programmes. Those that have been successful can demonstrate savings of up to 10 per cent of their energy bills. As waste removal and landfill gets more expensive, the less there is to be taken away, the less costs will be incurred. Reuse of packaging can reduce waste and save on purchasing costs. Reusing water resources is proving financially beneficial for some companies, particularly now that water metering is pricing water use at a more realistic level. Recycling materials and products can save money. Companies have discovered that proper management of paper, cardboard and metal wastes can generate small income rather than incur a cost for removal of waste materials. The benefits for organisations can be great:

> Dow Chemicals introduced many measures which led to a £3–5 million benefit and a 30 per cent return on investment.
>
> Xerox has established a recycling plant which has a turnover of £100 million per year.
>
> ICI's wash-water recycling saves the company £100,000 a year with low investment.
>
> Conoco installed heat pumps at an investment of £14,000 which paid for itself in four years.
>
> Pilkington's 'housekeeping' will save the company £30,000 per year with no investment.
>
> (Figures from Environmental Resources Ltd.)

In addition, the implementation programmes that support such initiatives can change the way the company operates permanently. Such an approach to business change provides a powerful tool to harness the energies of management and staff to change the organisation from within. However, although many large companies are reaping benefits from improved environmental performance, large businesses also rely on smaller businesses, and they are using their purchasing power to influence their suppliers. Suppliers therefore, must change. Indeed the ability of smaller organisations to change is greater if properly directed. The metaphor of the 'motivated minnows' versus the whale is still true. Imagine the speed of turn you see in a school of fish changing direction, compared with that of the whale. There are major benefits to be derived from motivating many small companies to change.

One advantage for small businesses is the ease and speed of response to changes of management direction – an ability to respond to customer needs at a level where responsibility for action and the action itself exist. Feedback from small businesses in the BS7750 pilot programme, however, indicated other disadvantages:

- *Financial*: While there is a recession on why bother? – survival is the priority; there is a high cost of capital; the paybacks are long term; we have low profit margins and this poor bottom line, together with limited assets, makes us a poor lending risk when there is little finance around.
- *Resources*: Resources are limited in terms of manpower, technical knowledge and influence, therefore we need off-the-peg solutions.
- *Image*: Small organisations are unable to exploit the good PR that comes from such a project.
- *Advice*: Practical support and not theory is needed and the cost of expertise (consultants) is perceived to be high.

Yet 96 per cent of all businesses employ less than 20 people. They employ over a third of the private sector workforce and produce nearly a quarter of the total UK turnover. So it is vitally important we find ways to aid small businesses in progression towards better environmental management. The benefits are very clear. Even if at this time they are mainly the lessons of 'big business', they can be extrapolated by the smaller business. After all, our experiences in improving the quality of the environment show how important the behaviour of small business is.

Rick Kelly, former head of the scientific services department of the GLC, draws a parallel with cleaning up the River Thames. It took many small companies changing their actions in little ways to make a difference. The engineer on the shop floor was as vital as the director on the board. One large company changing was not enough.

There is a parallel here with the quality approach that will be clear throughout this book: the need to focus on the small things to improve the overall picture. 'Big business' concepts must be made to work for the benefit of small organisations. What is needed to help them is a simple, systematic approach to achieve the required environmental management standard.

CHANGING CRITERIA FOR SUCCESS

In simple terms, for many organisations resolving the environmental issue is a major factor in determining a successful future and continuing profitability. Whereas price has always been one of the principal motivators of purchasers' choice, increasingly the 'environmental probity' of the product *and* the manufacturer are likely to be deciding factors in purchasing decisions. To help purchasers identify those environmentally sound products there are 'green label' schemes around the world, including the EC eco-labelling regulation, published in 1992, which resulted in the development of the UK scheme.

Labelling products that reach predetermined standards for environmental impact on water, energy or waste is relatively simple for some products, difficult for others. More challenging is the definition and assessment of the environmental integrity of an organisation. How can one assess the overall environmental performance to arrive at a conclusion that this company is OK and that another company is not? Who can make such judgements and what will be the implications on passing or failing? The solution for many organisations is to look at the way **management** performs as the yardstick.

THE PRINCIPLES OF ENVIRONMENTAL MANAGEMENT

Guidelines and principles for good environmental management have been established and promoted by many national and international organisations: the International Chamber of Commerce (ICC), the Business Council for Sustainable Development (BCSD), the Confederation of British Industry (CBI), the Coalition for Environmentally Responsible Economies (CERES), the Chemical Industry Association (CIA), and the European Petroleum Industry Association (EUROPIA). These guidelines include various common elements:

- A Policy statement that indicates the organisation's overall commitment to the improvement of environmental performance, including conservation and protection of natural resources, waste minimisation, pollution control and continual improvement.
- A set of plans and programmes to implement the policy throughout the organisation, including the advancement of the programme through suppliers and customers.
- The integration of the environmental plans into the day-to-day operation of the organisation, developing innovative techniques and

technologies to minimise the impact of the organisation on the environment.

- The measurement of the environment management performance of the organisation against the plans and programmes – auditing and reviewing progress towards achieving the policy.
- The provision of information, education and training to improve understanding of environmental issues – publicising aspects of the environmental performance of the organisation.

All of these elements combine to provide a systematic and structured management approach to environmental performance which is the subject of this handbook.

This systemic approach can be illustrated by showing the organisation as a tiered structure; executive management at top, making strategic decisions and setting policy; middle management, interpreting the policy into specific objectives and targets; and operations staff, implementing the plans to achieve the objectives through operating instructions. Activities are implemented, controlled, verified and measured to achieve the plans. The progress towards the policy is audited to assess

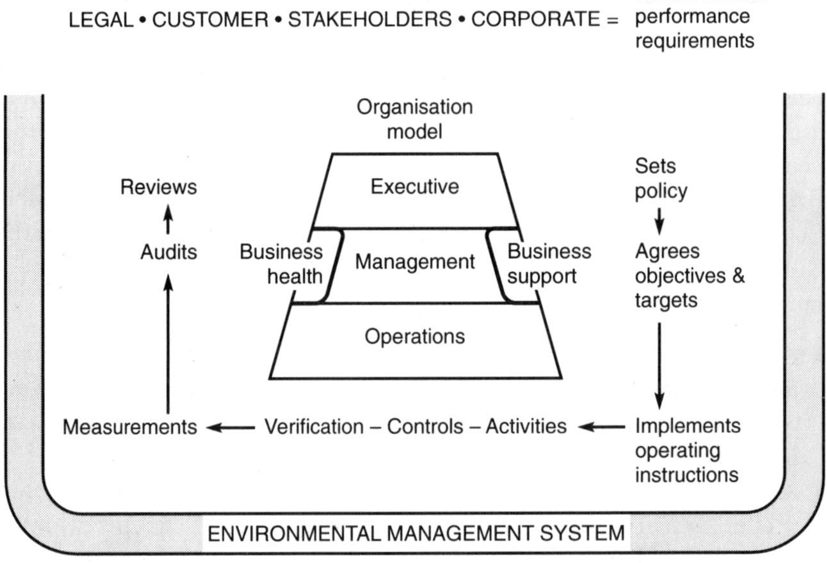

Fig. 1.1 Diagrammatic representation of environmental management system related to a business model.

conformity and executive management review progress and the audit results.

The environmental requirements are drawn from a wide range of sources: legal, customer, stakeholder and corporate. They establish the background of performance standards or criteria to be met.

MANAGEMENT SYSTEMS

How do you currently manage sales, purchasing, expenses, tax law, personnel, product design and performance? You do not leave these to chance, you would not survive in business if you did. So you take control, you define the requirements and put a system in place to meet them. Product requirements, set by the customer, can be addressed by a quality system. This system has management procedures in place to establish responsibilities, set targets, deploy resources, educate and train staff, monitor performance, audit the system, review and make changes to stay on track.

There is nothing new, therefore, in extending a management system like this, to address the environmental issue. What is new, however, is the focus applied to different elements within the system. The setting of standards for such structured management procedures is also not new. Such a structured management system concept exists in the field of quality systems.

Quality systems

Quality system concepts bring aspects of quality management to bear on all areas of the management system of an organisation. Quality in this context is the concept of *conforming to specified requirements*. A quality management system is the related policies, practices and procedures that are used to direct an organisation's activities towards meeting specified requirements. These are focused on the requirements specified by the purchaser of the products (or services) of the organisation subject to the contractual relationship between the purchaser and supplier.

The international standard ISO9000 (EN29000, BS5750) offers a model for quality systems, that is used in contractual situations between the purchaser and supplier of a product or service. Assessed compliance to the standard is used to assure a buyer that a supplier has the necessary management systems in place to deliver consistently the required standard of the product or service to meet the purchaser's specified requirements.

In the UK more than 15,000 sites of 11,000 companies are registered as having quality systems that meet the requirements of ISO9000 parts 1, 2 or 3. In relation to the 1.5 million firms registered for VAT returns, this may not appear significant. However over 90 per cent of VAT-registered firms have less than 20 employees, an indication that most large, and many medium-sized companies use or are familiar with such concepts.

Organisations that implement a programme to achieve certification to ISO9000 audit, review and change the organisations' management systems to ensure compliance with ISO9000 specifications. This need for change in the way an organisation is run, means that strong leadership is an essential precursor to success in implementing such programmes.

TOTAL QUALITY MANAGEMENT

Total quality management (TQM), supported by a new BS8750, takes the process of excellence in business management a step further, focusing beyond the quality management systems necessary for product or service delivery to meet specified requirements. Total quality management provides guidance for management philosophy and company practices that aim to harness the human and material resources of an organisation in the most effective way to achieve the objectives of that organisation. It provides process management tools that can be used to improve every part of an organisation, whether directly or indirectly focused on products or services.

Total quality management programmes, aimed at introducing these tools throughout an organisation, change the corporate culture to one that is externally focused, that is measuring its performance through the satisfaction of external customers, in contrast to those that are internally focused, measuring only internal performance indicators. An organisation's management system concentrates on analysing and redesigning every internal process and practice to become focused on customer-orientated measurements where the customer is the 'final arbiter' of an organisation's effectiveness and efficiency, the 'customer' being the recipient of a product or service, either inside the organisation (where some indirect service departments operate), or outside the organisation.

A key feature of the total quality management approach is the continual analysis, measurement and improvement through the quality loop which is illustrated in a simplified form in Figure 1.2. You can enter the circle anywhere, either thinking about a new process or product or measuring an existing process or planning for measurable improvement. The key thing is the 'never ending' search for improvement.

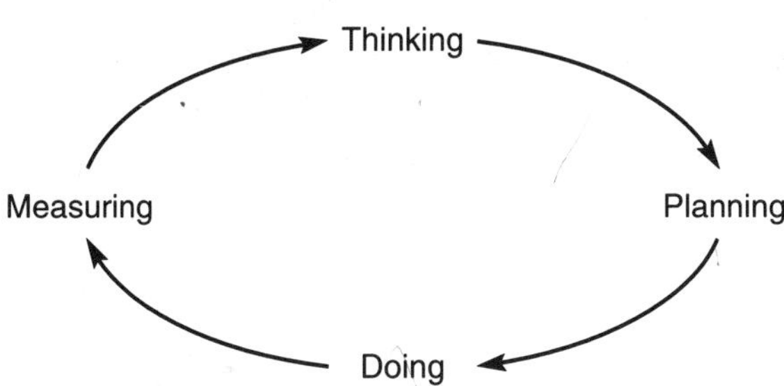

Fig. 1.2 The improvement loop

Think about what the goals are, the targets to be achieved, the route to be taken and the measurements to track success. Whether aiming at zero defects in a production process or no billing errors or discharge rates within a specified limit, this can only be achieved through the activities in the organisation. How will this be done?

Planning is the step to design the activities to achieve the goal. Who will have to do what, and by when in order to achieve the goal? What resources, skills and expertise are needed? What have we got? Is there a requirement for new resources, training and other steps?

Doing is the implementation of the plan. Striving to achieve the goal through simple, repeatable steps in an effective and efficient manner.

Measuring is the key to assessing the effectiveness of the *doing* stage. It assesses progress and focuses on the areas for improvement in the process. It leads to further thinking and refinement of the system. Do we need to do anything? What needs modifying or changing? What new measurements should be in place? The target is a constant 'honing' of the process to achieve even higher standards of performance, aiming at 'zero defects'. But we know that in life, things are not perfect. We can aim at a goal of 'zero defects', but as we approach milestones along the way, we

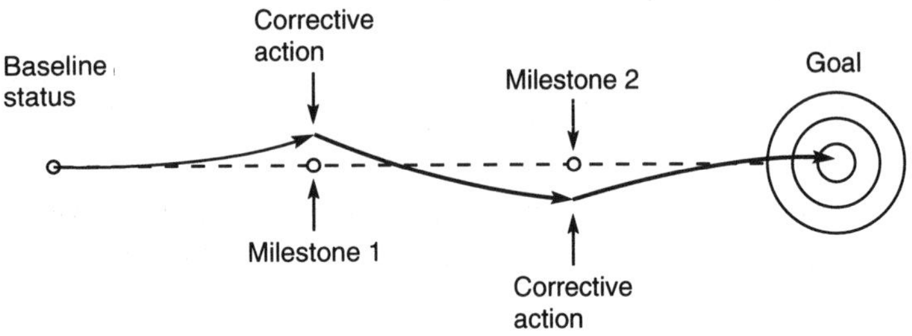

Corrective action
Baseline status
Milestone 2
Goal
Milestone 1
Corrective action

Note: Progress is off-course most of the time. Clear goals and milestones help corrective action to focus on appropriate adjustments.

Fig. 1.3

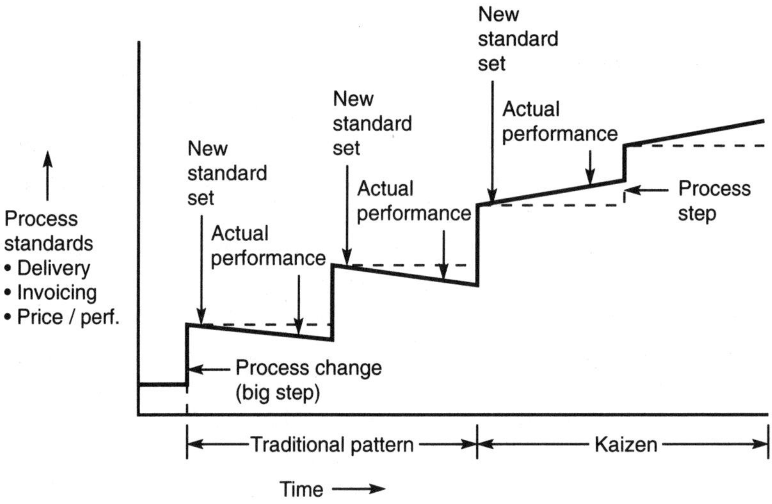

New standard set
New standard set
New standard set
Actual performance
Actual performance
Actual performance
Process step
Process standards
• Delivery
• Invoicing
• Price / perf.
Process change (big step)
Traditional pattern
Kaizen
Time

Traditional pattern – all 'workers' follow the new process and standards – process drift and lack of focus results in natural decline away from standard.

Kaizen pattern – all employees participate in the process improvement programme. Analyse the process, identify areas for improvement, make root cause problem solving assessment and implement problem solving techniques, changing the process marginally but continually.

Fig. 1.4

will see we are 'off-course', this is normal. The quality loop allows us to make changes to re-direct ourselves towards the target, through taking corrective action. See Figure 1.3.

Another way of looking at this continual pattern, is the Kaizen (small steps) approach. This encourages organisations to constantly review and improve small aspects of performance between major changes in performance standards and goals. It involves everyone in the organisation, participating in a positive way to improve the business performance.

About this book

The approach in this book follows a similar pattern to the quality loop. It provides a model programme for an organisation to use in *thinking* about, *planning*, *implementing* and *measuring* change in the way the organisation meets environmental performance standards. As a 'model' it is intended for use by any organisation, large or small, commercial or non-commercial.

I have assumed you are in the role of the environmental programme manager, charged with developing and implementing a programme to achieve a defined level of environmental management. In this case you are following BS7750 and the proposed EC Eco-management and Audit Regulation as the model and, using the four steps, *thinking*, *planning*, *doing* and *measuring* achievement. All businesses are unique. Therefore, the model is designed to be generic, although the implementation tools that are used allow management to ensure that the contents of the management system are relevant to, and owned by, the managers in the organisation.

We will aim at simple solutions, focused on clearly identified problems that are relevant to the global environment issues *and* your business. Energy management, waste control and reduction, reuse of materials and recycling, will figure, but the policy objectives and targets will be your own.

Along the way we will identify objectives at each stage, outline a method of achieving the objectives, and illustrate the text with practical examples. Because this activity is primarily an internal, management-led communication programme the success or failure of the communications is key. Communications in the workplace is based on the relationship between people, leaders and followers. Each section, therefore, will have hints and tips on communications.

PART I

■

Thinking about objectives: preparing for the planning phase

2

Thinking about the objectives

Before you embark on the programme of improving your environmental performance through a management systems approach, let me ask you a question – 'Are you serious?' The question has to be asked of yourself and the senior management of your organisation because in answering positively, you will need to accept the full implications of the approach.

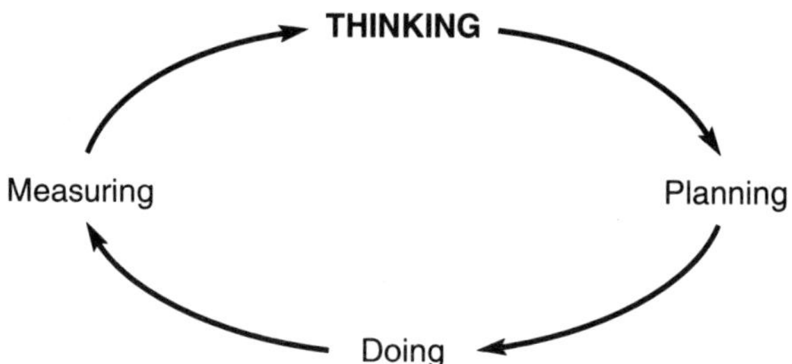

THINKING: Raising awareness and understanding.
Objective setting and completion criteria measurement.

Fig. 2.1 The 'thinking' part of the improvement loop

The environmental management systems improvement programme is a programme of *change*. It will, if properly followed through, require a re-examination of the value judgements made in the organisation. It will result in setting new objectives for *all* the business units, managers and staff. So if you are not serious and do not accept the implications of change, don't start. A half-hearted attempt to 'be green' while changing nothing about the way things are done in the organisation will fail, with the loss of credibility, resources and morale in the process. If you *are* serious, welcome to the start of 'the green road' that has no ending.

OBJECTIVE

The objective at this early stage of the book is to set the scene for the subsequent planning and implementation phases by improving understanding of:

- **the environmental performance issues;**
- **the environmental management standards;**
- **the environmental management system elements.**

The environmental performance issues

The Earth is an integrated and isolated system. Over a period of time there are cyclic changes in the Earth's patterns and movements that are quite normal. What we have realised recently, underlined by the potential impact of the depletion of the ozone layer, is that man can have a lasting and far-reaching impact on the Earth's systems.

Of the various global issues of global warming, pollution and raw material depletion, the most significant is related to climate change and greenhouse gas emissions. These have the capability to raise the temperature of the Earth's surface with potentially damaging consequences in food supplies, crop patterns, flooding, drought and other abnormal weather patterns. The ozone reduction risks potential damage from radiation currently reflected or absorbed.

The principle greenhouse gas emissions (CO_2/CFCs/N_2O/CH_4) are related to energy production and fossil fuel use. With 20 per cent of the World's population accounting for 75 per cent annual energy use, the industrialised world has significant responsibility in this area. The developing world anticipates a population growth that has significant potential impacts on demands for energy and fossil fuel use.

Deforestation is another significant source of impact on the global environment. The burning of large tracts of forest and the loss of oxygenating material provides a dual negative impact. In addition such

Table 2.1 Greenhouse gas emissions by region 1985

USA	21%	Other developed countries	27%
Rest of OECD	23%	Eastern Europe/Russia	22%
China and Asia	7%		

Table 2.2 Contribution of each greenhouse gas to global warming 1980

CO_2	55%	CFCs −11 and −12	17%
CH_4	15%	Other CFCs	7%
N_2O	6%		

Table 2.3 CO_2 emmissions by sector

Buildings	36%	(heating 43%; appliances 20%; cooling 14%; lighting 14%; water heat 9%)
Industry	32%	(machine drive and electricity 32%; steam 27%; process heat 19%; oil 7%; HVAC and light 6%; feedstocks 6%; plant 3%)
Transportation	32%	(automobiles 43%; light trucks 20%; heavy trucks 14%; aircraft 14%; rail/marine 7%; non-oil based 2%)

Source: *Changing by Degrees*, The Congress of United States Office of Technology Assessment, US Government Printing Office, Washington DC, February 1991.

activity reduces significantly the diversity in animal species and the resulting monoculture crops do not support the rich variety of indigenous species.

Pollution from the industrial processes can cause damage that, although shorter lived than the potential impact of global warming, can cause health and environmental damage on a large scale resulting in long-term damage to the natural assets of society and the planet. Through acid rain, again related to energy production from power stations, forests and water courses have suffered long-term damage and degradation.

Raw material use has to be balanced to ensure that limited precious sources are conserved. Whether mineral extraction, foresting valuable open lands, stripping hardwood forests or fossil fuel use, the ability of the eco-system to replace and recover is limited. The demands that consumers place on the suppliers needs to be modified to reflect the sustainability.

In looking at the environmental performance of organisations, therefore, all aspects of industrial activity, buildings and transport have to be considered. These affect all parts of the organisation and the environmental management system that will provide the control for improved environmental performance must encompass all these issues.

The environmental management standards

The environmental performance issues show that it is possible to look at your organisation's environmental performance relative to the global issues – the 'think global, act local' philosophy. The environmental management system standards approach brings together three concepts:

- Everything we do in business has some impact on the environment.
- Management systems control everything we do in business.
- Standards can be set for environmental management systems.

The environmental management system is the means to control and improve the environmental performance of the business. It is the mechanism to ensure that you have in place the necessary controls to *understand* the environmental performance required; to *measure* your current environmental performance against that requirement; to *identify* where areas for improvement planning exist; and *implement* the improvement plan through, controlling and tracking your critical activities to achieve the desired results. *You* require the environmental management system to be:

1. fully integrated into your overall management processes;
2. contributing to improving overall company performance;
3. recognised as appropriate by those people most interested in your environmental performance.

ENVIRONMENTAL MANAGEMENT TOOLS

Before looking at the elements that go together to make up a comprehensive environmental management system, it is useful to understand other management tools used for improving environmental performance that may form part of the integrated environmental management system.

1. **Products:** There are schemes for labelling products that meet predetermined environmental performance criteria, established through a product *life-cycle analysis*, e.g. batteries that are mercury free. The UK is about to launch its scheme under the EC Ecolabelling Regulation.

2. **Projects:** There is a requirement for major construction projects to undergo an *environmental impact assessment* procedure, this is enacted under UK planning laws promulgated by the EC Directive on environmental impact assessment.
3. **Sites:** Many organisations have used a form of audit to assess activities that have an environmental impact. This *environmental auditing* is quite common in the petroleum and chemical industry sectors where, because of the nature of the product, processes and complex regulations, management requires close control of environmental performance. Environmental auditing has been defined as:

> A systematic, documented, periodic, and objective evaluation of how well environmental organisation, management and equipment are performing with the aim of helping to safeguard the environment by (i) facilitating management control of environmental practices; (ii) assessing compliance with company policies, which would include meeting regulatory requirements.
> (International Chamber of Commerce)

THE ROLE OF STANDARDS

There are standards for all of these management tools to ensure effective implementation: standards against which products are to be tested to acquire an eco-label, established by the relevent competent body managing the scheme; standards for the scope, the process and the technical content of environmental impact assessments established by the regulators; and standards for environmental auditing practices and procedures established by industry and consultant trade associations. One of the benefits of having standards is that they provide a common basis on which to compare the performance results of different products or systems. Standards can be used inside an organisation to self-assess compliance with a requirement and they can be used by those outside an organisation as a benchmark of good practice – an important factor when public information about the environmental performance of an organisation is accepted as key to a sustainable development philosophy.

A model or standard for environmental management systems, therefore, will provide a useful tool for an organisation to use in controlling its environmental performance effectively and providing a basis for external recognition. Furthermore, a standard on environmental management systems that could relate to the existing Standard in quality systems (BS5750) would provide an *integrated* approach that would allow organisations to demonstrate both a product/service performance and an environmental performance compliance capability. This is the basis for BS7750: A Specification for environmental management systems, a new British Standard that establishes a generic model for any organisation that is compatible with the requirements of BS5750: quality systems, but separate from it, to allow its independent application and assessment.

BS7750 provides a general, or generic, guide to good environmental management systems practice. It does not identify the specific environmental performance criteria expected in any particular company or industry sector. The issues faced by a large chemical company are not those faced by a small printing works, tannery, local authority or hospital. For industry, therefore, it may be appropriate to relate the generic standard to sector environmental performance issues. Such sector guidance could provide help in two areas:

- to those inside an industry about the issues to address in the policy and practices of the organisation; and
- to those outside the industry who wish to assess the implemented system against the Standard and a model of good practice that is relevant to that industry.

THE PROVISION OF INDUSTRY-SPECIFIC GUIDELINES

In setting environmental performance targets within the organisation, therefore, you will want to ensure that these are relevant to your industry and the Standard. You will want to ensure that your response is consistent with the current, and possible future, requirements of the Environmental Protection Act (EPC) and Integrated Pollution Control (IPC) schedules.

IPC introduces the concept of BATNEEC, 'the best available techniques not exceeding excessive cost', intended to ensure that there is a cost-effective benchmark of good environmental performance within industry sectors. BS7750 therefore recognises the possible use of complementary sector application guides. These can ensure that issues which face particular industries are recognised and incorporated into the environmental target-setting of companies in those sectors. For example, the extract from the Loss Prevention Council document 'Pollutant Industries' contains an appendix – Pollution: High-Risk Industries and their Pollutants (see Fig. 2.2) This shows the particular

INDUSTRY¶	*TYPE OF WASTE PRODUCED*	*PHYSICAL FORM*¶	*OTHER INFORMATION*
Agriculture, Horticulture‡ (0100)	BOD Waste (high & low) Disinfectant Pesticides, herbicides (see below) Fertilisers	L S A A P A A	These include wastes from animal husbandry. Silage effluent can be 200 times more polluting than untreated sewage, cattle slurry 100 times more. In England & Wales, 17% of pollution incidents in 1988 were attributable to farming.
Coal distillation Coal tar (2512/2567) Coke ovens (1200)	Ammonia Aromatic hydrocarbons Combustion products Cyanate Cyanide Dust Fluoride Hydrocarbons (general) Hydrogen sulphide Phenols Polycyclic hydrocarbons Sulphur dioxide Tar Thiocyanate	G A G L G A G A S P G A G L A G L A G G G L S A	Certain sectors of the coal industry will come under integrated pollution control for air pollution control. Other sectors will come under local authority control for air pollution. Gaseous emissions are the main concern.
Construction, Building, Demolition (5000)	Combustion products Asbestos Dust Metals Rubble Timber	G P S P S S S S	Dust nuisance especially during demolition. Building sites often have a container that can hold 500–1000 gallons of diesel for site vehicles. These are rarely bunded (sealed) and spillages often occur giving problems.
Electrical, electronics (33/34)	Copper Mercury Organic solvents Precious metals Selenium	S L G L S S	Metals are essential to this industry, and the presence of these in waste effluents may bring the industry under integrated pollution control. Organic solvents are widely used for cleaning and emissions will need to be reduced, although recycling of the solvents is normally carried out.
Electricity generation‡ (1610)	Clinker Combustion products Cooling water Pulverised fuel ash Nitrogen oxides Sulphur dioxide	S G L S P G G	It came under integrated pollution control on 1 April 1991, and all new plant will require authorisation under the Environmental Protection Act. Concern over nitrogen oxides and sulphur dioxide
Fibres, Textiles‡† (43)	Bleach Cyanide Detergent	A A A	The detergent waste is mainly anionic, but some cationic effluents occur (cationic detergents are non-

Fig. 2.2 Extracts from Appendix 2. Pollution: High-Risk industries and their Pollutants (IPC document)

types of waste produced by industries and their physical form. An assessor examining the environmental management system of an organisation in these industry sectors might reasonably expect that such recognised industry issues would form a prominent place in the environmental performance targets.

Trade associations or federations often facilitate these sector guides, e.g. British Association of the Construction Mining Industry (BACMI) provides an environmental code for its industry members which includes a phased programme to set up an environmental management system from establishment of a corporate environmental statement to external reporting on performance.

The environmental management system elements

One of the environmental management tools we looked at earlier is the environmental audit, which included facilitating management control of environmental practices. The audit does this by identifying areas where environmental performance is failing to achieve the required standards and recommends management actions to correct the situation.

If it is possible to define the shortcomings in a management system that addresses environmental issues, is it also possible to define what such a system should look like? What elements, activities, practices or procedures should be established within a system for managing environmental performance?

The Chemical Industries Association's (CIA) 'Responsible Care' guidelines, the ICC charter and the CBI Environmental Forum provide models. Similarly, the Norwegian government, Canadian Standards Association, Netherlands Confederation of Industry (VNO) and now the EC Eco-Management and audit Regulation provide such elemental guidance.

WHAT ARE THE ELEMENTS?

BS7750 brings the elements together in the world's first national standard for environmental management systems. The elements are described in more detail in Appendix I, but broadly include:

Commitment from the top of the organisation. Key to the success of the application of an environmental management system.

Preliminary review which establishes the baseline of environmental performance, the primary areas of environmental effect and the opportunities for improvement.

A statement of **environmental policy** which summarises the organisation's commitment to and direction for environmental performance management.

Methods for understanding the requirements: environmental effects procedures, including tools to analyse the environmental impacts of the organisation's activities to ensure that the system is focused on the critical areas for consideration:

1. A *cradle-to-grave analysis* which identifies the environmental issues related to a product, from the procurement of raw materials through the manufacturing process and on to the use and disposal of the product.
2. A special approach to projects and the *environmental impact assessment* of other major decisions within the organisation, prior to the commitment to a course of action.
3. An *environmental management communication process* which identifies environmental issues throughout the organisation, involving all business activities and staff.
4. A method for identifying the *regulatory and other interested parties' requirements* to be met by the organisation in its activities, leading to the setting of environmental objectives and targets throughout the organisation.

Environmental quality system – a supporting quality system to ensure that the environmental performance objectives and targets set as a result of the effects analysis and the regulatory requirements are met. The system should include:

- A system audit and review procedure to ensure that the environmental quality system and related environmental performance are meeting the specified requirements.
- A reporting method to inform those with an interest in the organisation's environmental performance, of the achievements that have been reached.

With all of these elements in place, adequately documented and implemented to a recognised standard, the organisation should be assured that the required environmental performance is being met. Relevant to global issues.

CHECKLIST

- *Have you established a reading list of material to establish a base-line knowledge?*
  - *Georg Winter,* Business and the Environment, *McGraw-Hill, 1988.*
  - *'Corporate Quality/Environmental Management: The First Conference', Global Environmental Management Initiative (GEMI), Washington, 1991.*
  - *Coopers & Lybrand Deloitte/Business in the Environment,* Your Business and the Environment – A D-I-Y Review for Companies, *1991.*
  - *International Chamber of Commerce,* The Business Charter for Sustainable Development.
  - *Environment Strategy Europe, 1991. Including WICEM II official report, Campden Publishing Ltd. EC Eco-Management and audit Regulation.*
- *Have you reviewed the environmental impact of the organisation's activities at the highest level?*
- *Have you looked at the current management system status in relation to quality systems or any other quality programme approach?*
- *Have you read through the environmental management system standard BS7750?*

3

Preparing for the planning phase

Now that you understand more about the environmental issues and environmental management system standards, you need to understand the nature of the change that is required, the organisation's capacity to make the change effectively and the steps to implementation.

OBJECTIVE

The objective of this part of the book is to set the scene for the overall programme. Think about the investment requirements, the management issues, and the outline plan.

The investment requirements

What are you likely to be investing to achieve the status of an integrated environmental management system to a specified standard? Quality is free, and there is no doubt that in the long term investment in improved quality systems does pay for itself in reduced costs and risks of failure. Similarly, many examples have shown that the investment in *environmental* quality programmes brings real benefits in energy, waste and resource savings and reduced risk of legislative breaches. The investment required is in the areas of:

- management resource;
- time allocation;
- training; and
- financial investment.

Management resource includes the allocation of a senior *management* representative to oversee the programme as part of his or her responsibilities. He or she will act as the project owner and director, responsible for policy and other strategic issues. You will allocate responsibility for implementation to a *project manager* who will implement the policy that has been agreed at a senior level. In addition, all managers will need to commit resource to learning and communicating the new approach.

All managers and staff will have to devote *time* to learn the new challenges and invest in planning improvements as the cascade of information throughout the organisation takes place. Time must be taken to attend the awareness and implementation workshops and to follow-up on the activities subsequently identified. These activities will be in the area of documenting practices and procedures, environmental system documentation and implementation.

Training will be a requirement for all the managers and staff to help them become aware of the issues and to equip them with new skills to resolve the issues in their day-to-day work routines.

Some *financial* resources may be required if you propose to employ outside resources for some of the preliminary environmental review activities. Financial investment may be required as a result of your investigations to achieve identified improvements in activities or business processes. These will be costed as any proposed business investment, and assessed on their merits.

As an example drawn from the BSI pilot programme, a small business working group identified a potential 100 hours' consultancy time and 750 hours' 'company time' spread out over a 12-month programme.

The management issues

One of the steps advisable at this early thinking stage is to check that the organisation is capable of making the changes necessary to achieve the new goal, and to assess the organisational skills required to carry it out. This 'coherence check' (see '*Testing a Company's Power to Implement*' by W. Paul Krasse and Ed de Sa Pereira) will provide information you need before you start the planning of your project. All the business elements of the organisation must be checked, but in particular the *skills* available within it, as these will enable you to understand where the main inhibitors to progress may lie, and plan to deal with them.

A report is needed for management to understand the overall status of the organisation's capacity to accept the proposed change management programme.

ACHIEVING AN INTEGRATED SYSTEM

One way of looking at an organisation as an entity is to break it into its elemental parts. This has been done in the past by McKinsey using a seven-element approach. The alliterative technique of the 7-S helps us to understand the importance of the linkages between *all* the elements in an effectively functioning business organisation.

The elements of the 7-S model are shown in Fig. 3.1. Each element needs to meet the needs of the shared purpose and the other elements, to create a balanced management system.

- **Shared purpose** – captures the goal or mission of the organisation.
- **Strategy** – comprises the business plans of the whole and parts of the organisation to achieve the shared purpose.
- **Structure** – identifies the integrated roles and responsibilities for parts of the business.
- **Systems** – comprises the business process, practices, procedures or activities that result in outputs towards the business goals.
- **Staff** – are the people in the organisation, their status and areas of activity.
- **Skills** – are needed to implement the shared purpose, either provided by staff or outside resources.
- **Style** – is the way managers and staff behave and use time, and are recognised and rewarded by the organisation.

All the elements of the 7-S model need to have appropriate consideration when designing, developing or analysing organisations in order to make changes. One of the common causes of failure when organisations implement changes is the lack of integration between the business elements during the change process. We are all familiar with different scenarios:

- A new accounts system or a new ordering system is introduced, but the staff are inadequately trained to bring their skills up to the necessary level for maintaining the system. The system is then criticised for failing when the answer may lie elsewhere.
- A company sets out a new strategy but fails to change the internal styles and reward systems to reflect the new direction. The organisational reward system may still be encouraging behaviour to meet the needs of the old values.

As the manager responsible for implementing the environmental management system, you are introducing a new strategy that will

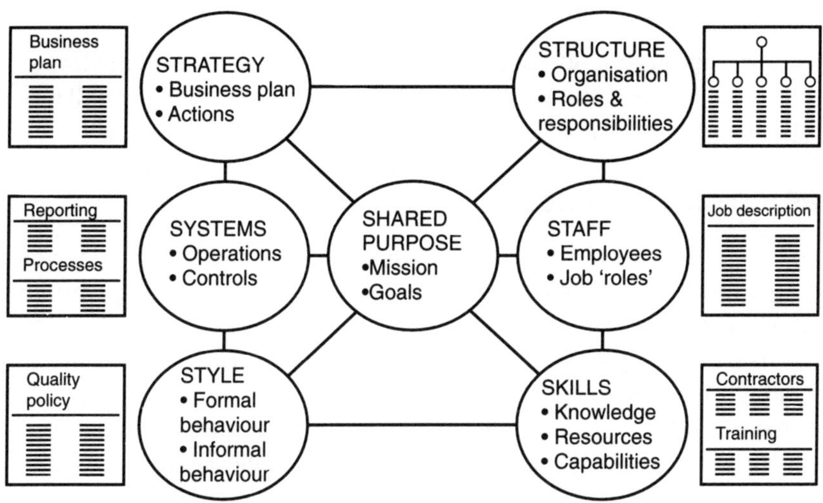

McKinsay 7–S model of business elements. All the elements will be impacted by the change management process.

Fig. 3.1 Elements of the 7-S model

require some change in *all* the business elements. You will assess and adapt the 7-S elements to meet your circumstances.

- **Shared purpose** – to include improved environmental performance as a common goal of desirable behaviour, captured in the policy.
- **Strategy** – To ensure that environmental performance criteria are integrated into the business plans of the whole and parts of the organisation.
- **Structure** – To ensure that environmental performance management roles and responsibilities are defined and allocated.
- **Systems** – To ensure that the day-to-day practices and procedures implement the environmental performance standards.
- **Staff** – To ensure that appropriate staff are identified to enable the smooth implementation of the environmental performance standards.
- **Skills** – To equip staff and have access to the necessary skills required to implement the environment performance standards.

- **Style** – To ensure that managers reflect the environmental performance standards in the way they behave and use time, and recognise and reward their staff activities.

When changes are made to all of these elements and the elements are integrated in consistent support to the shared values, then you will have high confidence of achieving your goal.

THE 'COHERENCE CHECK'

The 'coherence check' consists of a review of the elements related to your organisation, but with particular focus on just two: the strategy and the skills. The review of *strategy* is to understand the current direction of the organisation, and to relate that to a changed strategic approach that includes environmental management as a new consideration. The review of *skills* is to understand the capacity of the organisation to achieve the transition. Without the relevant skills being available, a focus on other elements may fail if the staff are inadequately trained to accept and implement the changes required.

So you must now arrange a series of interviews with the senior managers, using the 7-S model to discuss the current status of:

- the current business activities;
- existing business development plans;
- the possible implications of the introduction of environmental management systems;
- the availability of skills to facilitate the transition; and
- other business elements that have particular relevance.

The result will be a composite picture of the current business, the overall strategic direction of the organisation, and the areas of concern in implementing the environmental management system. Interpretation of those results should allow you to focus on the terms of reference of the project – what you are going to do, what you are not going to do; the general timescale, costs and resources required; the priority of the project; and the scope of your responsibilities.

The project quality system

As project manager, you will need the freedom and authority to make decisions about project resources, and actions by others you are dependent upon.

It is important to clarify these responsibilities as a part of the project documentation, and the most appropriate way of approaching this is to develop a project quality plan. This will contain a number of elements that you must document and to which you must obtain agreement, namely:

Objective: Agree the mission, scope and extent of the project activities; then implement an EMS on XYZ site.

Strategy: The overall plan to achieve the objective; from preliminary review to audit and assessment, the major activities.

Dependencies: What are you dependent on to achieve the mission?; the project team, resources, commitment, staff and systems.

Deliverables: What you will deliver in achieving the mission; workshops, communications, system documentation and an auditable system.

Procedures: The detailed procedures to be developed for implementation; checkpoints, reporting, detailed timetable and instructions for participants.

Measurements: What will be measured: progress against plan, workshop satisfaction and use of resources.

Change Control: How will changes to the project plan be implemented; what change control procedures or error correction?

An outline of these elements of your project in a single document will assist you in clarifying the position of the project and the roles and responsibilities of the key participants.

The outline plan

The objective here is to attain a measurable goal through a project programme. A project must have:

- unambiguous completion criteria (you will know when you have finished);
- unambiguous success measurements (you will know how well you did it!);
- a definite life span (a start and an end); and
- a defined organisation.

The completion criteria will be conformity to the environmental management system standards BS7750. The success measurement will be the assessment of compliance to the Standard through the internal audit, and eventually, external certification. The timescale will depend on the organisation's size, complexity and activities, as well as its capacity to change. The 'organisation' will include definition of the roles and responsibilities of the senior management representative, the implementation project manager and the project implementation team, the new roles for staff and managers at a generic level, and any additional specialist resource.

PROGRAMME PHASES

The programme will have several phases:

1. Management review and approval
2. Planning and set-up
3. Preliminary review
4. Awareness through line management
5. Implementation through line management
6. Project review

Management review

Management review is the presentation of the 'coherence check' and agreement to the scope, resources and criteria of the project.

Planning and set-up

Planning and set up is the phase of bringing together the implementation team, confirming the mission and detailed programme development workshop.

Preliminary review

Preliminary review is a formal review of the environmental risk, opportunities, strengths and weaknesses.

Awareness programme

Raising awareness is achieved through the design and implementation of a presentation for cascading information throughout the organisation.

Implementation programme

The implementation programme is achieved through the implementation workshop. This is designed to involve discrete business units, departments or functional managers with common reporting lines. They will be encouraged to review their current business activities in the light of the requirement to address environmental management issues. Implementation workshops are reviewed in greater depth in chapter 9.

Project review

The project review is the activity to assess the completeness of the project and the attainment of the project goals. It will include self-assessment and preliminary audit results.

As an example, a small firm in the BSI pilot programme showed the following steps:

Preparatory review (8 weeks)
Familiarisation/fact finding/data collection.
Policy formulation (4 weeks)
Scope/ethos/focus/style.
Systems set-up (12 weeks)
Manual/procedures/training.
System implementation (28 weeks)
Primary and secondary procedures/operational control.
Systems auditing (16 weeks)
Training EMS auditors/in-house verification/external mock certification/QA check.

The total programme ran for some 52 weeks with phases overlapping.

CHECKLIST

- *Have you considered the investment requirements and explored the potential inhibitors?*
- *Have you carried out the 'coherence check' and report?*
- *Have you analysed the skills capacity to change?*
- *Have you identified which decisions are yours and who else do you need agreement from?*
- *Is everyone committed?*
- *Have you a complete picture of the organisation?*

COMMUNICATION HINTS

- Embark on a brief but comprehensive 'listening campaign'.
- To get a picture of the 'state of the art' attend seminars, read papers including BS7750 and the proposed EC Eco-Management and Audit Regulation, documents and books, talk to your peers and competitors, use the Confederation of British Industry, the Institute of Directors, Business in the Environment, your trade association and the British Standards Institution.
- Tell everybody all the time about the importance of the work. Do not understate the involvement and commitment that is required. Treat the programme as the serious, professional project that has significant implications on the future of the business that it is.

4

BS7750
Some questions and answers

Some common issues were raised in the pilot programme, and at various conferences and meetings which developed BS7750. Some of these issues are addressed here in a question-and-answer format. They may help you to focus on the issues of EMS implementation that are relevant to you.

1. Does it help to have BS5750? Is it an essential prerequisite?

BS7750 was designed to 'stand alone'. You do not need BS5750 certification as a prerequisite. The approach to BS7750 uses the same concept of a structured quality system, but is set up to assure specified environmental performance goals. Organisations that have BS5750 find it relatively easy to extend their management systems to address the BS7750 requirements. Many of those approaching BS7750 directly find the structure and approach well presented and 'good common sense'.

2. How do you obtain management commitment from an environmentally disinterested board?

Take some time to analyse current issues in the organisation – particularly financial issues related to waste and energy use – and assess potential savings. Check if the customers are thinking environmentally. Assess the potential risks for loss of business. Check if new or planned legislation may have an effect on the organisation's activities. Assess the potential threats of non-compliance. If, when you present your findings, you get a 'nice but we don't have the time or resources' response, draft out your CV!

3. How do you put a boundary around the register of regulations? Won't it be huge?

All organisations need some process to ensure that they stay within the law. It may be by using professional experts, consultants or qualified staff, or by using documentation and continuous professional training programmes. The Standard requires documentation *relevant to* the environmental aspects of your activities. This means important consents, planning consents or restrictions, discharge limits and regulations that require a specific or particular response over and above day-to-day compliance.

4. How do you put a boundary around the environmental effects analysis? Isn't this endless and therefore impossible?

The use of the word 'effects', sometimes makes you feel it means all the possible consequences of any behaviour, after all everything we do has some environmental effect – even breathing. The key factor here is the test of *reasonableness*. What would be reasonable in the eyes of those outside the organisation?

The initial 'scan' around the organisation can ask function, business and departmental managers to self-assess overall effects and identify those as 'significant' against predetermined criteria. Ways of limiting the extent of an effects analysis vary depending on the problem. It can be where your product ceases to be identifiable – if it is used in another process or changed by the next process. There is no hard and fast rule. I never like giving an 'it depends' answer, but in this case it is true. Ask yourself, 'Is it reasonable for the particular tool being used, e.g. life cycle analysis, to stop here?' Should it continue to the next step in the process? What happens if the store has a fire, the chemicals were combined, or the aluminium sulphate was placed in the wrong tank? Where does the water waste go, the solid waste end up? Is my contractor properly authorised and registered?

5. How do you identify a significant issue?

The Standard focuses on significant issues to limit the objectives and targets to relevant and achievable goals. In particular, it focuses on two factors related to the activity: product and process.

(a) Do they relate to global issues? For example,

- Global warming: energy use or 'greenhouse' gas emission;
- Resource depletion; waste minimisation and sources of materials and choice;
- Pollution: discharges, emissions and waste streams.

(b) How significant are they within the operation?

If you are a manager at an IBM UK plant like Havant, for example, the management issues may be related to CFC phase-out, or energy and waste streams at high level; however, if you are a fencing contractor, in addition to material supply source, you may well consider the choice of wood preservatives you use in your business.

6. If the manual is going to contain all the information on how I run the business, won't it be huge?

If you have no other management manual, at first sight the requirement seems daunting. The intent however is to bring together in one place all the key elements of the systems you use so that you, your organisation and third parties can see that you have a comprehensive system. It is a place to put unique documentation like a policy statement and an organisation roles and responsibilities diagram. It is not the place to repeat the documentation on the Control of Substances Hazardous to Health (COSHH). The manual should signpost where other documents are to be found and who the owner or maintainer is. In this way it can be readily seen that a process exists, and where it can be found and who owns and uses it.

7. Objectives and targets sound OK, but you don't really expect detailed quantification, after all some things can't be measured?

Statisticians will tell you that most things can be measured. The goal is to put some measurement on all the significant activities and processes, even those you feel today have been unmeasurable. Some companies create measurement scales or estimates drawn from available data on a simple, empirical scale to set a baseline and start to measure for improvement. The key is to establish a measurement system and then improve both the process being measured and the measurement system in the light of the information gained.

8. Can my organisation comply with BS7750 for part of the organisation (main production processes) to satisfy a third party, without applying it to its own in-house activities?

No. One of the critical elements for success in the approach to environmental management under BS7750 is the 'whole organisation' requirement. It encourages a more holistic approach to the issue, because that is the only way to address some of the environmental issues we face. It does allow the definition of 'organisation' to go down to a small level, including a site, but not to separate a process from the organisation that supports it.

9. Training raises many questions. Do I really need to run a new training programme? What should be the main learning points in the education plan? What is the most effective approach?

There is a need for a training programme to make people aware of the issues. Then, if you want to do things differently you will need to involve them in applying that awareness to their jobs. The main learning points are suggested in chapter 10. There are benefits in integrating the environmental training into the main company programmes, providing the specific learning points are addressed in the revised content.

10. How do you make the environmental policy statement public?

Some companies use the annual report (for example, IBM), others make special arrangements including publicly available documentation (for example, Norsk Hydro, Hereford City Council). The critical point is that everyone in the organisation knows the policy exists and can refer to it.

11. Where does the preparatory review stop? This could be an endless activity like the effects analysis.

The main aim of the preparatory review is to identify those areas that the EMS should focus on. The SWOT analysis format will provide the overview to highlight the areas necessary for inclusion in the policy and that will require more detailed analysis under the environmental effects analysis.

12. How do I commit my organisation to continuous improvement when many of the environmental effects are governed by mechanised processes difficult to improve without substantial investment?

The focus of BS7750 is continual not continuous improvement, a conscious committee decision. Compliance does not require improvement everywhere in the organisation every day. It does require a continuing programme of improvement that, over a period of time, demonstrates that a reduced burden is being placed on the environment. Today, it may be improvements in energy management; tomorrow in waste minimisation; in six months, a planned investment will reduce water usage. One change may result in an increase in, say, gas consumption, with a decrease in electricity consumption. This may provide an overall improvement in environmental performance as part of a continual improvement programme.

13. My company is very busy trying to survive in the middle of a recession (or the middle of a rapid growth situation). Where do I find the resources and time to implement an EMS?

Lack of time and resources are the most frequently heard reasons for doing nothing, and familiar to those responsible for the quality programmes in many organisations. As quality guru John Deming said, 'You don't have to do this, survival is optional!' Try to make the programme relevant to you and your position. Focus on the small steps, and progress by integrating the activities into the day-to-day business of your organisation. Reward those who deliver real benefits to the bottom line. Whether you are struggling or very successful, improved profitability is worth the investment.

14. What happens if I don't achieve my objectives and targets? Will I lose my certificate? What about the bad publicity?

There is a risk that failure to achieve objectives and targets in a significant way may result in deregistration and, consequently, bad publicity. Such an approach should reflect the value of the registration and the credibility of those in the scheme who do achieve their targets.

Experience with quality systems assessment shows that appropriate recognition of system failure, followed by subsequent corrective action does not jeopardise registration. However, persistent breaches would be viewed differently. It is specified in the Eco-Management and audit Regulation that any breach of legislation will result in deregistration, through links between the legislators and competent body.

15. How should I carry out audits? Should I use internal staff or must I use consultants?

There is no 'must' about the use of external consultants for system design or internal audit. Consultants provide resources that would otherwise not be available in an organisation. They can also provide a broader perspective with their wider experience. Internally trained staff have more knowledge about your business than an external consultant and you retain the skills in the organisation.

Qualifications for assessors/verifiers calls for independence from the organisation being assessed. This usually means an assessor from an appropriately accredited body. However, the Eco-Management and audit Regulation indicates that the individual verifier could be internal, providing he/she was independent of the business area being assessed, and suitably accredited.

16. How will assessment and certification work? Will this be by my BS5750 assessor or by a new organisation with all the attendant extra costs?

As skilled as your BS5750 assessor may be, experience in environmental auditing has shown that he/she is unlikely to be competent in areas specific to environmental performance, methods of measurement, testing, and legislation. The skills needed for an audit team to assess effectively an EMS are:

- quality system assessment skills;
- environmental skills; and
- industry skills.

The latter are to ensure that appropriate issues are being considered by the EMS in relation to the standards of your specific industry. These skills can be obtained by training staff experienced in other skills or by team building.

17. What does 'abnormal working conditions' mean?

Unlike an accident, incident or emergency conditions which are uncontrolled, abnormal working conditions refers to activities that are controlled but occur infrequently. Because they are unusual occurrences, risks of system failure may be higher and special actions may be needed to ensure the environmental policy and practices are not put at risk. Examples include start-up and shut-down procedures wherever people are unfamiliar with the routines and standards expected, or where the systems are untried and untested, and refurbishment or construction activity.

18. What should be the scope of 'emergency plans'?

Emergency plans should be established as a result of a formal risk assessment procedure to identify, in a structured manner, those anticipated risks within the organisation. Some eventualities have a higher probability than others. These should be planned for, including discussions with outside agencies.

However, major incidents like Flixborough, Piper Alpha and Exxon Valdeez, show that the consequential events beyond the first, possibly predictable, event can have far-reaching consequences. The incident and accident management systems therefore need to have flexible responses but clear roles and responsibilities in terms of communications, actions and reporting. Lessons from such events can then be learned quickly and passed on to reduce future risks.

19. Who will artitrate appropriate policy, objectives and targets in an EMS?

The technical committee responsible for BS7750 felt that the most appropriate body responsible was industry itself, through trade associations and federations which could identify the significant environmental issues in their industry, and document these in sector application guides (SAG). The guides would identify the particular issues of energy management, waste or pollution control that are relevant for a specific industry. It is these issues that should be addressed in the environmental policy, and the objectives and targets of the EMS of an organisation in that particular industry.

PART II

▪

Planning the implementation of the environmental management system

5

Obtaining commitment and establishing the team

At this stage you have established a core of information about environmental issues generally, a basic knowledge of the environmental standards you wish to implement and a picture of your organisation's readiness to develop and implement an EMS standard strategy. You now need to acquire agreement at board level to proceed to develop a plan, agreement on the scope of the plan and the resources needed to build the implementation team, agreement on the timetable of implementation, and of course, a project plan.

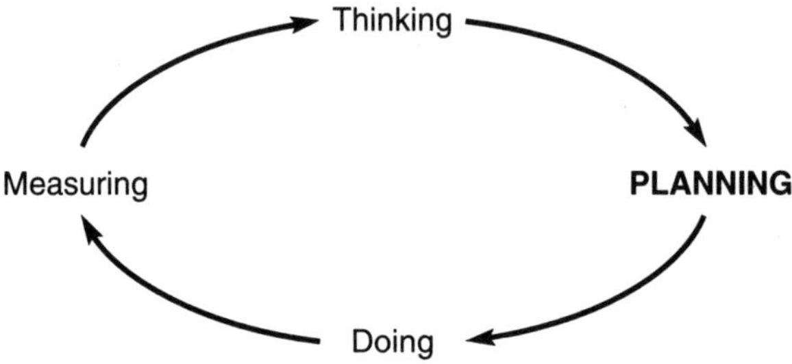

PLANNING: Establishing the project plan, the route map to the objective.

Fig. 5.1 The 'planning' part of the improvement loop

It is essential to gain the commitment from the top of the organisation to ensure the environmental policy is integrated into the management structure, the decision-making processes, resource allocation, priority setting and business measurements (to name a few), without which you will not achieve the integrated environmental management system you desire. So how do you get that commitment? Whose authority do you need?

The communication impact matrix (see Fig. 11.1 in chapter 11) is important in designing the communications process correctly to achieve the desired output. In this case the ongoing objective is to raise awareness of the issues at senior management level and obtain agreement to specific proposed course of action.

OBJECTIVE

To raise awareness of the environmental issues which affect your organisation and make a specific proposal for action, addressed to a senior management level.

Raising awareness in your organisation

Raising awareness is done through two steps in this plan. Firstly a formal presentation is made to executive management to obtain approval for the programme design and give the authority to act; secondly, having established the project team and carried out the preliminary review to 'benchmark' the current environmental performance, a presentation is designed to be cascaded by line management prior to the implementation workshop activity.

What information is likely to interest senior management?

- Recent environmental court cases, relevant to the organisation's activities and the implications on its liabilities.
- Recent or planned environmental legislation that directly or indirectly will affect the organisation's activities.
- Inquiries or pressure from customers and consumers that may impact future profitability.
- Industry or community 'peer pressure' that may identify threats or opportunities.

Having collected your information to raise awareness, you may now make a more formal presentation to the board on the way forward.

Planning the presentation

Book yourself on to the agenda of a relevant management executive meeting and plan your presentation. You could entitle the paper 'Environmental Standards: an issue for us?', or whatever is relevant to you with your knowledge of the business. Consider what the desired outcome of your presentation is. Not only awareness and understanding, but also the commitment to a course of action. If you want agreement you must be firm about the four Ps: *position*, *problems*, *possibilities* and *proposal*.

You must put a firm *proposal* to the executive team. The senior managers will know that there are choices to be made – in which direction should the organisation go, how far, how fast and with what resources? As with any project such *possibilities* must be explored. To agree to explore the options suggests you have made a clear *problem* statement – one that is relevant to the organisation's profitability, image or legal status. The problem will need to be put into context if it is to have meaning to the senior management team, and this is the *position* statement which should introduce the presentation.

The proposed running order therefore is:

Position

Where are we now? What are the outside events that may affect your organisation?

- Legal background
- Stakeholder interests
- Insurance
- Customers
- Corporate drivers
- Community or peer pressure
- Banks
- Staff
- Competition

What is the internal status of your organisation?

- Environmental performance
- Incidents
- Staff awareness
- Finance
- Accidents
- Risks
- Management skills
- Resources

Include also highlights of current environmental performance; existing management system status; Control of Substances Hazardous to Health (COSHH); investment programme; projects; initiatives.

Problems

Why should your organisation bother to improve its environmental performance?

- What we know/don't know
- The lack of cohesion and direction
- Lack of recognition or priority
- Products/services not being developed
- The failures that exist
- Cost of failure
- Savings not being taken
- Recognition of opportunity

Your organisation also has the opportunity to change its culture, to introduce or reinforce its drive for quality.

Possibilities

- Do nothing! In the light of the above, is it business as usual? Then what?
- Do everything! Do what? What are the priorities? What should be invested? What will the impacts be?
- A balanced, cost-effective solution, which will be appropriately managed to a measurable conclusion, e.g. compliance to BS7750 or the Eco-Management and audit Regulation.

Proposal

The seven steps towards achieving environmental standards.

1. Obtain executive commitment today to set up the necessary project team, resources and organisation.
2. Carry out a preliminary review of the company's status and report back to the board.
3. Establish an outline environmental policy and obtain executive approval.
4. Establish a detailed action plan, for awareness and implementation of the policy, and obtain approval.
5. Communicate the plan; through 'awareness' presentations.
6. Implement the plan, through 'implementation' workshops.
7. Measure the success of the plan and the environmental improvement.

At this point you must become the 'active listener'. Although the champion of the proposal, in the end it is the task of the executive managers to make the decision. They have to 'own' it. They will discuss, probe and dig to see if you have done your homework and got your facts right. Particularly on the predictive part of the presentation – 'What if the Eco-Management and audit scheme does not prove essential? 'What if the environmental issue goes away?', 'How do you know this will become a major issue?'. You must answer these questions honestly. You will not always know the answer, and an 'I don't know, but it seems to me that . . .' answer is usually the best approach.

You must be flexible in responding to ideas about changes to the plan providing they still meet the objective. But be firm. You must not compromise on the impact the plan will have. The executive managers must be fully aware of the implications and accept them. It is a management change programme and *will* have significant impact.

Having got your authority to proceed you can now establish what activities must take place and set up a team to undertake these activities.

Establishing the project activities

To implement the requirements of the project you will need to be aware of the activities which will have to take place. Table 5.1 shows the activities and the stages at which they will be employed in the EMS implementation programme. You will notice that some of the activities address more than one requirement, eg implementation workshop.

Management meetings are needed to agree scope, programme, policy, status and future action plans of the EMS. These can be specific meetings or extensions of existing management meetings. The choice depends on your view of the most appropriate route that will achieve success.

Awareness presentations are needed to set out the position and direction of the programme. Interactive sessions help to share the current state of knowledge and to introduce the problems that will be faced. No attempt is made in this stage to develop solutions; every attempt is made to highlight the benefits in pursuing the policy of improved environmental management.

Table 5.1 The activities needed for the EMS implementation programme

Requirement	*Activity*
Management policy	Management meeting
Organisation and personnel	Awareness presentation Implementation workshop Performance planning Job objective setting
Environmental effects	Implementation workshop Performance planning EMS documentation
Programme	Implementation workshop
Management manual and documentation	Implementation workshop
Operational control	Implementation workshop
Records	Implementation workshop
Audits	Self-assessment exercises EMS audit
Reviews	Management review meeting report

Implementation workshops are needed to develop the response at a departmental level. Interactive sessions are used to explore the activities to be implemented and the contribution that each department can make to the business goals. Implementation workshops can also explore the areas where activities and procedures can be changed to meet the environmental performance challenges.

Self-assessment exercises can be used to allow managers and staff to measure their progress in implementing the EMS.

An environmental management system skeleton must be documented to provide a framework for departmental activity and to analyse practices and procedures. The contents of the framework is provided by each department through the implementation workshop.

Job objectives are needed to define the roles and responsibilities for staff that manage or perform work related to the environmental policy, objectives and targets.

Performance plans are needed to set specific achievement objectives for those who perform work related to environmental policy.

EMS audits are needed to assess the compliance of the system with the Standard's requirements so that the management activities and procedures meet those requirements and that the system elements are effective in meeting the environmental standards requirements.

Management review meetings are needed to monitor progress and performance and to establish an improvement programme related to the current EMS.

The implementation workshop is the main tool for establishing the departmental environmental management system as it will be documented in the common skeleton that you provide. It may be that your organisation already has a documented quality system in place that provides a local framework for objectives, practices and procedures. In that case you will be adding to the contents of that system, to ensure integration of the EMS into the existing management system. The EMS then becomes a 'thread' running through the organisation. It is tied into the day-to-day activities, practices and procedures and is integrated into the reporting, objectives setting and rewards systems. The EMS, therefore, will be just as simple, or as complex, as your current organisation.

Establishing the project responsibilities

To illustrate the typical structure of the project approach, the roles and responsibilities are as follows:

- *Executive management*: The senior management body in the organisation – the board or committee responsible for running the organisation own the environmental policy and programme.
- *Management representatives*: Members of executive management responsible for the implementation programme, through the EMS project manager.
- *EMS project manager*: Line manager responsible for implementation of the project plan, leader of the project team.
- *Project team*: Project support team drawn from all parts of the organisation. Each representing a department or function to ensure ownership and co-operation throughout the organisation.
- *Line managers*: Managers responsible for discrete areas of activity or process within the organisation. Responsible for the performance

management of others. Will need to identify environmental co-ordinators or representatives in their area of control.

- *Departmental environmental co-ordinators*: Responsible to a line manager for understanding, co-ordinating, supporting and representing the department in activities related to the project programme.
- *Internal auditors*: Staff trained in audit skills, to support the EMS audit activities. These may be departmental environmental co-ordinators, or other staff, when auditing they must be independent of the area under review.

Establishing your project team

Key to implementing the communication and workshop programme is the project team which should be drawn from the management departments and staff groups. The project team is the main resource for getting the message out to the people on the ground, your local 'champions'. Who should be in your project team and what should they be responsible for?

An important member of the team is the *environmental programmes manager* who is responsible for delivering the project, i.e. you. You are likely to provide the secretariate and general co-ordination activities. You will need a chairperson who is the executive sponsor or *management representative*. (This may still be you in a small organisation.)

You will need a representative from each *line management function* – from the production, manufacturing, maintenance, marketing research and administration departments. You must have a representative from each function, even if the manager's initial response is, 'This does not apply to me!'. All parts of the business have some environmental effect, and all aspects of the business interact with one another, so if the change management programme is going to be successful, you will need full participation.

If you have a *quality programmes manager* responsible for the BS5750 programme, you will need his or her support to integrate the requirements into the existing documented systems. If you have education and communications staff programmes, you will also need the support from these departments to help design and integrate the messages in your organisation's training and communication.

The next step is to develop a coherent plan of action that is 'owned' by your team members. To do this, you will develp and involve them in a workshop to establish a common view of the goal and the critical factors to succeed in achieving the goal.

CHECKLIST:

- *Have you planned your presentation to obtain agreement with the senior management? Position, problem, possibilities and proposal.*
- *Have you established support at the highest level of the organisation to your plans?*
- *Have you considered the relevant environmental issues that will provide interest for your senior management.*
- *Have you checked the activities for each part of the programme?*
- *Are your team complete with representatives from each key function?*

6

Action planning: a team workshop

You have agreement at high level to implement the overall programme, now you need support across the company from the people who will be responsible for seeing it through.

The managers in the organisation, therefore, need to have a voice in the plan to implement the changes. This is done through the representation on the project team, and it is important to establish consensus for the project plan with the team, so that they feel they 'own' it, when reporting back to their constituencies.

OBJECTIVE

The goal is to obtain agreement on the detailed action plan for implementing the EMS to the agreed standards.

Creating a plan with the project team

The first stage is to bring together the *project team* members. It is essential that the team has an agreed mission also the activities necessary to achieve the goal, the priorities of those activities and the allocation of resources to meet those activities. The critical success factor (CSF) technique is the best method to use to reach a consensus on the mission statement and the activities that will be necessary to achieve the mission. A successful project plan can be attained through a CSF workshop.

The critical success factors

The objective of the workshop is to enable a team of people with a common goal to agree what the priority activities are, and therefore where resources should be focused. It does this by introducing the concept of CSFs, which help identify key actions in a positive and co-operative way. The approach has been successful in helping teams plan projects, improve departmental business processes, functions and organisations.

Critical success factors provide a link between the mission, which is clear unequivocal and measurable, and the activities necessary to achieve the mission. The mechanism employed is based on a consensus approach. After that, analysing and agreeing the activities to achieve the CSFs is (relatively) painless and becomes a (comparatively) straightforward exercise.

To be 'critical' in importance there must not be too many of them. Indeed, more than eight and they begin to stray into a general statement of wishes. By keeping the factors to eight or less, we can be confident they really matter.

Each CSF must be precisely focused on one element. It is not sufficient to say, 'We must have senior management support and the skills necessary to implement the programme'. This statement incorporates *two* CSFs which may both be critical but which may require different activities to implement them.

Each CSF must be fundamental to achieving the mission and each must be a *measurable* achievement or an 'achieved state'. For example, if your mission statement is

> 'To establish an environmental management system in [company name] by [date] that meets the requirements of BS7750 and the Eco-management and audit Regulation.'

Then the statement, 'We must have senior management commitment to the programme' is a CSF because without senior management commitment our mission will fail. It is measurable because we will know when we have achieved senior management support.

So the approach is to set up a meeting of the project team to develop the CSFs and the action plan. Attendees will be *all* the team – all the members must be present, if they are not available, change the date. One of the key factors for success in this kind of exercise is consensus from all the participants, so do not hold the meeting without everyone there.

A technique for deciding the project plan: a CSF workshop

STEP 1: AGREE THE MISSION!

A brief statement of one or two sentences summarising what the team are jointly going to do. That sounds easy, but experience shows that what you may think you have agreed is not the goal that the rest of the team have in mind. Sometimes 'hidden agendas' appear at this stage. This is just as well; clear them up now and be prepared to listen and react to comments and suggestions until the mission is agreed. It must be by consensus, but of course it has to be in line with your terms of reference. Get this wrong and all the rest of the activities that follow will be wasting resources.

STEP 2: WHAT ARE THE DOMINANT INFLUENCES ON THE MISSION?

Hold a ten-minute brainstorming session to answer this question. Anything and everything that could influence the achievement of the mission can be mentioned. The usual rules apply.

BRAINSTORMING RULES

- Ten to fifteen minutes at the most, briskly led.
- Everybody should contribute, in orderly fashion, but you can 'pass'.
- Anything can be said no matter how lateral it may appear!
- Nobody can challenge or question other contributions.
- No more than two word concepts – not a speech!
- Keep track on a flip chart.

The material which results from the brainstorming session forms the core from which you will draw out the CSFs. All the dominant influences have implications on the mission, but as you examine them, some will be more critical than others. The dominant influences can be grouped under the categories of the 7-S model (see chapter 3) to ensure an even spread of factors.

STEP 3: LIST THE CSFs

We now use the brainstorming material to create the CSFs. We know the mission and we have an idea of the dominant influences that may impact the achievement of the mission. From that we can list the factors critical for success. Remember the list should not exceed eight essential points if the exercise is to be successful, each starting with 'we must' or 'we need'.

Take a point from the dominant factors and see what was meant by it. How critical does the team feel it would be to the achievement of the project. Develop a sentence that best captures the 'achieved state' to be desired. Keep working at it until the team agree, by consensus, that the sentence is right. This is your CSF. Then proceed to take another dominant influence and so on. Do not fall into the trap of adding 'just one more'. Keep pressing the team to choose the really *critical* factors among all the things that could affect the mission.

An alternative method is to divide a flip chart into eight boxes and then place the dominant influence of similar themes into a particular box. Such a technique avoids the left-over syndrome. Using this method for example, would mean that all the items relating to training and educational skills would appear in a single place.

Example

A workshop group at Brunel University performed an exercise to establish a list of CSFs. Having completed a brainstorming session the group's list included the following:

1. The team
2. Resources
3. Open Minds
4. TEB (totally enthusiastic boss)
5 Committed GOGs (guys on the ground)
6. A plan
7. Standards
8. Roles and responsibilities

The full CSFs were developed to look like this:

BRUNEL MANAGEMENT PROGRAMME: ECO-AUDIT AND ENVIRONMENTAL MANAGEMENT SYSTEMS

Mission: 'Putting in an EMS to meet BS7750'

Critical Success Factors:

1. We must have an appropriately skilled team.
2. We must have a resource plan to meet the mission.
3. We must have open minds to accommodate change.
4. We must have a 'TEB' (totally enthusiastic boss).
5. We must have committed 'GOGs' (guys on the ground).
6. We must have a plan.
7. We must establish standards/targets to aim for.
8. We must identify roles and responsibilities.

Other CSFs might include the following:

- We need to ensure that our staff are trained to understand the implications the company's environmental policy, objectives and targets.
- We must ensure that the environmental programme is integrated into the day-to-day practices and procedures to be effective.
- We must demonstrate market advantage from our proposed investment in improved environmental performance.
- We need to establish an effective quality system to monitor and continually improve the implementation of the environmental management standards programme.

As a quality check, you can go back to the 7-S model in chapter 3 to check for completeness but do not be surprised if one or two elements are thought not to be critical. It may be that skills, ownership and planning are key right now, and that style and systems are seen to be less so. Your original *coherence check* (chapter 3) will probably have confirmed that.

STEP 4: DECIDE ON THE ACTION TO BE TAKEN

We now have a group who agree the mission, and the critical factors necessary to achieve the mission. From here it is a relatively straightforward step to decide on the actions necessary to achieve the CSFs.

On a separate flip chart write the CSF across the top of a page. You need four columns: action, owner, date and measurement.

Action. Define an activity which is necessary to achieve the CSF. You can brainstorm the activities if it helps. Check with the group that you have all the actions necessary to achieve the CSF.

Owner. Acceptance of ownership implies taking responsibility for implementing something. You might experience unwillingness to accept ownership but the team has agreed that certain things need to be done, so identify the owner whose role in the organisation best fits the task in hand. For example, if the task is an issue of communication, then ownership should be the responsibility of the representative of the communication department, if it's a training issue, the training department's representative has ownership. Make sure the tasks are shared out so that everyone is interdependent on each other to succeed. It helps later on. Do not take all the actions yourself. You are the project manager not the entire team so share the ownership.

Date. It is no good having an open-ended action to be implemented. You need to know when the action needs to be completed and set a date. Be careful to set reasonable targets: too far ahead and jobs never get done; impossibly short and you lose credibility.

Measurement: You will all need to understand the completion criteria for the task. It needs to be relevant to the subject, but it can be fun. If gaining executive management approval to the plan is an action, a documented minute will do. However, gaining approval from the training manager for the workshop plan, might be measured by a blue rosette! Employ techniques that will lighten the meetings and make them worthwhile and fun to attend.

Now you have a plan for one CSF, go through the rest. You will find the first a bit slow to do, but as you progress a momentum gathers and it leads you through the last CSFs quickly. Record the actions to be taken for each CSF, alone with the owner, date and measure in a table such as that shown in Table 6.1. You will also find that some actions appear on more than one CSF. This is to be expected, and repetition of such an action indicates that it is probably a critical activity.

STEP 5: CONSOLIDATE THE RESULTS INTO A COMPREHENSIVE ACTION PLAN

You should now ensure that the actions are clearly noted by the team participants. Your job is to take away the results and consolidate them

Table 6.1

Action	*Owner*	*Date*	*Measurement*
Draft plan for review	MJG	1 Nov	To agreed criteria
Senior management review and comment	Departmental representatives	1 Dec	Response, 3 Dec
Revised plan to senior management	Departmental representatives	14 Dec	Documented
Present plan to senior management meeting for approval	MJG	21 Dec	Minuted
Publish and communicate	MJG	28 Dec	House Magazine

into a comprehensive action plan for the team, in a form that they can present back to their sponsoring departments. This is the core of the project plan you have set out to achieve. Like all plans, however, it is only as good as the information presented. To keep it current and relevant as a control tool you need to track progress against the plan and adjust it whenever things slip or accelerate. The team will then regard the plan meetings that you will hold as essential.

CHECKLIST FOR SUCCESSFUL PROJECTS

- *Terms of reference must be clearly established:*
  - *What is the desired outcome?*
  - *Who is responsible for what?*
  - *What are the criteria for decision-making?*
- *The project manager must have an appropriate balance of responsibility and authority to achieve the desired outcome.*
- *The project must be supported by a team with an appropriate balance of skills and resources.*
- *All the team members must have clear objectives.*
- *There must be a plan to achieve the objectives.*
- *A tracking mechanism should monitor the progress to the plan:*
  - *Where are we?*
  - *Where should we be?*

- *A control mechanism should be in place to change the plan should it be necessary.*
  - *What needs to be done?*
  - *Who is responsible?*
  - *How will you know it has been done?*
- *There must be a communication process to keep everyone informed of progress.*

COMMUNICATION HINTS

- The output from this workshop provides material to report to the executive management team on the agreed way forward. Use the opportunity to reinforce the mandate you have been given to clarify the actions that now have the support of their nominees.
- If you have an in-house newspaper or magazine, use some of the material to publicise the project start-up, the project team members and the outline of the plan to begin the awareness process.

- Ask your project team members for confirmation that they have reviewed the material with their own area of responsibility to ensure the messages are getting back to the line managers.

Part III

▪

Implementing the environmental management system

7

The preliminary review

The preliminary review is the first stage of the 'doing' part of the EMS implementation programme. It is intended to establish a benchmark of your environmental performance. It will help you to design the awareness presentation to be cascaded throughout the organisation, and set the agenda for the implementation workshop programme which is key to integrating the environmental management system into your company management system.

The awareness presentation will be designed by you for use throughout the organisation by you and/or the project team members, a suggested outline of the presentation is given at the end of this chapter.

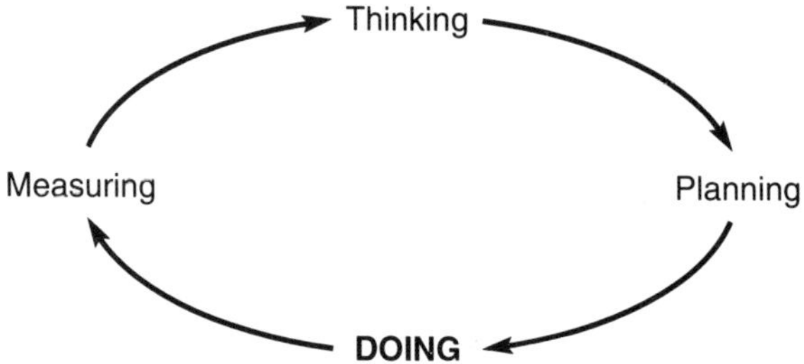

DOING: Implementing the plan and progressing towards the objective.

Fig. 7.1 The 'doing' part of the improvement loop

The implementation workshop is an interactive activity carried out with a manager and his subordinate team, which may be a board, a management team or a manager and his reporting staff. It is described more fully in chapter 9. The preliminary review is often referred to as the 'searchlight sweep' around the organisation in order to highlight those areas where more detailed analysis will be required. It is the first of the environmental audit type of activities. It is a structured, systematic programme but not designed to test an assertion or measure against a standard. It is a fact-finding review of the whole organisation.

Note: Because the term environmental audit has so many different uses, it is not used by BS7750. The standard refers more precisely to the *preliminary review*, *environmental management system audit* and *environmental management system review*. All of these are a form of environmental audit.

The product of this stage of implementation is a report which will recommend actions for improvement. The core of the report will be a form of SWOT analysis. The process of the preliminary review is to look at *all* the aspects of the organisation. Where relevant it should extend beyond the business boundaries to look at suppliers, purchasers and the product life cycle. The report which results from the review will provide guidance on the areas of significant environmental effect, so it must consider all parts of the organisation and all activities. The report should contain the following elements:

- An appraisal of current environmental policies and practices.
- An appraisal of current performance.
- An outlook on environmental issues and implications.
- A SWOT analysis – the strengths, weaknesses, opportunities and threats.
- A list of recommendations:
  - the principal objectives and goals;
  - a plan;
  - a timetable; and
  - the costs and benefits.

OBJECTIVE

The goal is a report that will be presented to the project team and executive management. The report will assist the project team in achieving the CSFs by defining the plan to implement the environmental management system standard providing data for communications and measurements for progress tracking in the future.

The SWOT analysis technique

This technique analyses strengths weaknesses opportunities and threats of the whole organisation.

STRENGTHS

The strengths are those areas of system control or performance that are positive. For example, having BS5750; a strong pollution control process; new plant or equipment; non-contentious products or services; high levels of skill; a committed senior management. These are areas to build-on in developing and moving forward.

WEAKNESSES

These are areas where system control or performance appears at risk: where practices, procedures or processes indicate some opportunity for failure. Some examples might be: Breaches of legal compliance; the risk of significant exposure should a failure occur; poor materials management; the use of hazardous processes with inadequate controls; a lack of operating instructions; a lack of emergency plans; a lack of clarity in the ownership of the process. These are areas that the action plan will focus on.

OPPORTUNITIES

These are areas where new actions or initiatives may bring benefits. For example, the introduction of: new products; new services; new processes; skills training; management leadership programmes; links to product quality; links to total quality management (TQM). These will need to be followed up in the action plan.

THREATS

These are risks which may not be clearly apparent but which may damage the short- or long-term development of the organisation. Examples could be: changes in market circumstances; new laws being developed; the effects of changes in consumer demand; the effects of change in supply sources; social or community pressure; or stakeholder risk assessments by banks or insurance companies. These may need policy formulation before actions are implemented.

Conducting a preliminary review

The key to carrying out a preliminary review is to treat the activity as a project. Like all projects it should comprise:

- *A thinking phase* – Define and agree the scope and objectives; set unambiguous completion criteria.
- *A planning phase* – define a schedule; plan your organisational requirements, resources, methods, roles and responsibilities.
- *A doing phase* – Implement an information gathering programme; evaluate and report within a specified time frame.
- *A reviewing phase* – agree the actions arising from the report.

There has to be a plan to get from the start to the finish of the review, it should be, designed to achieve the objectives, clearly and unambiguously laid out. A tracking mechanism is needed to monitor progress towards the objective and a control mechanism is required to change the plan if there is a problem.

Defining the scope of the review puts a boundary around the assessment. Decide where you will go and where you will not. For example, are you reviewing the whole company, the whole of site X, or the whole life cycle of product Y. Agree an outline timetable and the measurements for completion.

Setting objectives ensures that the team is focused on what it will produce and when, so that effort goes only in the area required.

Defining the schedule and planning your organisational requirements, resources, methods, roles and responsibilities sets out how the project will be carried out. What people, finance or equipment do you need?

Implementing the information gathering programme provides you with the raw data you will need for the review. Assess the data and put the results into an initial report. Be careful to stay on programme.

Agreeing the actions arising provides you with a follow-up procedure to implement the report.

SCOPE AND OBJECTIVES

Agree the objectives and limitations of the assessment. Which parts of the business have a priority or are likely to be the focus of the review? Is there a time constraint? What are the expectations at the completion of the project? What resources are available?

In discussion with the team, agree who will be the core personnel to carry out the review. You may choose to delegate this to a small sub-team of 2–4 people who can have access to all areas of the company. Ensure that the team have the right levels of expertise, for example have they project skills, technical skills and process knowledge?

SCHEDULE AND RESOURCES

Plan out the resources available against the areas to be assessed, so that all the team members know who is responsible for what. Having mapped out the programme, get all the team together to discuss and agree the way forward.

Preliminary review: meeting agenda

- Introduction and background
- The project scope and objective
- The plan of work
- Who is doing what
- How it will be done
- Communications – in the team
  – outside the team
- Report plan

It is useful to provide a 'role data sheet' to each team member so that each knows, precisely what they are to do and where they are to do it. For some areas you will have to define how to obtain the data – the methodology.

Interviews will form the main source of information. Talk to key personnel about the operations and activities. Checklists allow you to ensure that all the information from the interviews is in a common format.

INTERVIEW CHECKLIST

- *Indicate your three to six main activities.*
- *What are the objectives?*
- *Who or what are you dependent upon?*

Activities	Weeks 1	2	3	4	5	6	7	8	9	Ownership
Scope	XX									FB
Schedule and	XX									
resources	XX									All
Checklists	XX									MH
Questionnaire	XX									MH
Communicate		XXXX								TO
Action										
Management			XXX							MH
Area 1			XXXX							FB
Area 2			XXXX							CG
Function 1				XXX						FB
Function 1				XXX						CG
Data Collation		XXXXXXXXXXXXXX								MH
Draft report					XXX					MH
Reporting										
Team review										All
Management	XX			XX				X		All
Executive	XX			XX				XX		MH
							XX			
Follow-up										
Urgent items										
Agree action plan										TBA
									XX	All
									XX	

Fig 7.2 Preliminary environmental review – plan

- *What is the output?*
- *What are the environmental effects?*
- *What are the levels of energy use, waste, discharges or emissions?*
- *What raw materials, paper, transport are used?*
- *What are the legislative issues?*

Questionnaires can be useful but the rate of return is low. Use a telephone interview if the data is critical and the contact remote.

In other areas, you are looking for data on consents; energy bills; existing practices and procedures; measurements; reports inside the organisation; guidance from trade associations or consultants' reports; and documentation from regulatory authorities.

To ensure that you get the support you need from all staff let them know clearly in advance about the activity and the possible contacts and interviews. Bring the team together at regular intervals during the review to compare progress against the plan. Follow-up and be willing to change the plan if a new area or direction seems valid as a result of the interim meeting. An example of such a plan is shown in Fig. 7.2. The aim is to ensure that all main activities have a place in the programme and that each has an owner and can be allocated an appropriate amount of time and resources.

ACTION

You are now ready to go out and gather the information you have identified as necessary. Implement the plan; fill in the questionnaires; carry out the interviews; and track down the data you need. There are four key areas.

- **Legislation and regulatory requirements:**
  - Current legal obligations and consents?
  - Future regulations?
  - European influences?
  - Product legislation?
  - Communication with regulators?
  - Marketplace legislation?
  - Waste controls?
- **Environmental effects/processes/products/risk areas:**
  - Energy management and use?
  - Heat, light and power?
  - Raw material sources?
  - Pre-production processes?
  - BATNEEC analysis?
  - BEO analysis?
  - Transport and distribution?
  - Types of waste Storage? Volumes? Disposal methods?
  - Duty of Care compliance?
  - Recycling or reuse status?
  - Suppliers' performance?
  - Consumers' management?
  - Water quality and use?
  - Discharges?
  - Product design?
  - Packaging?

- **Environmental management practices and procedures:**
  - – Environmental policy?
  - – Environmental strategy?
  - – Communications?
  - – Public relations?
  - – Investment plans?
  - – Procurement policy?
  - – Project assessments?
  - – Environmental records?
  - – Environmental audits?
  - – Environmental systems?
  - – Environmental responsibilities?
  - – Training and skills base?
  - – Community pressure?
  - – Insurance and indemnities?
  - – Materials and equipment supplies?
  - – Product assessments?
  - – Environmental reporting?
  - – Environmental reviews?

- **Feedback from previous accidents or failures:**
  - – Non-compliance records?
  - – Accident reports?
  - – Contingency plans?
  - – Progress of action plans?
  - – Incident records?
  - – Emergency planning?
  - – Emergency response training?
  - – Communication strategy?

REPORTING

Before the data starts to come in, prepare the report structure and format. This will allow you to allocate the data as it comes in into the right sections for summary analysis.

Gather the data from the team as it is generated. Check that it makes sense, is factual and accurate. Review any areas of serious concern with the manager of the area to allow him or her the opportunity to start any remedial actions immediately.

Do not be judgemental. The report should state *facts* which are supportable by evidence. Summarise your conclusions and propose recommendations for action where there is a clear way forward. Wherever possible identify what the problem is, and what should be done to initiate improvement actions. Do not provide a solution but indicate a direction to be taken for a solution to develop. Identify the ownership of the problem and the resources and timetable for resolution. Suggest relevant standards for achievement or models as examples and any other information that is relevant. If areas need further investigation that will take you outside the scope of the review. Identify them and include them in the recommendations for further action.

Discuss the findings with the team to ensure that there is a common understanding of the issues, criteria and priorities, and with the managers and those who participated in the review. Your objective on publication of the report is that there should be no surprises!

The presentation to the executive team should be preceded by forwarding a copy of the report for review. This can be followed by individual meetings if the results are likely to be contentious. Formally present the report at the executive management meeting. Use a summary set of OHPs and talk for no more than fifteen minutes. The talk should cover:

- What the scope was;
- How it was done;
- Thanks for co-operation;
- Conclusions in full;
- Recommendations and an explanation of the priorities.

Allow time for discussion of the recommendations and ensure that a clear direction is given. There can be several outcomes of the meeting:

- The agreement and acceptance of all the recommendations. (Well done!)
- The agreement and acceptance of most of the recommendations but a modification of the time and resource effort that will be needed to implement the recommendations.
- The non-agreement and rejection of the recommendations, but approval to undertakc more review work. (OK, but get clear terms of reference for the new programme.)
- The non-agreement and rejection of the recommendations and a refusal to undertake more review work. (Project completed. If you have managed to achieve all the project objectives, Well done!)

FOLLOW-UP

Assuming you have been successful in achieving agreement on progress so far, you must now implement the follow-up programme. The first steps are to ensure that any areas where urgent action was recommended are acted upon immediately. The second is to publish the report, or a summary of it, as part of the awareness communication programme. This provides a powerful launch to the initiative and the facts and figures usually make fascinating reading. Then invite the owners of the actions that have been approved to a meeting to kick-off the second phase of the implementation plan which will result in the establishment of policy, the setting up of a management organisation, the definition of roles and responsibilities.

Examples

Hereford City Council's preliminary environmental review produced a substantial set of documents. They were based on the following three documents: (a) BS7750; (b) 'Environmental Auditing in Local Government' (1991) by the Local Government Management Board; and (c) the briefing sheet 'Environmental audits of local authorities: terms of reference' (1990) by Friends of the Earth.

The exercise was carried out as part of the BS7750 pilot programme. It was managed by the internal environment project manager, who was supported by internal officers and seven man-months of external resources. The set of documents that were produced comprised: (a) a register of environmental effects and audit; (b) a register of regulations: (c) a register of recommendations; and (d) an environmental summary.

The external cost to Hereford City Council was about £18,000, with a similar amount from the 'internal' budget. The documents were reviewed by the Council and are now publicly available. An extract from the Recommendations follows.

---

25) A management plan should be produced for the River channel and bankside of the River Wye. This could include a) the identification of acceptable or unacceptable developments or activities in relation to the River so as to maintain its conservation interest, b) establishing the potential for habitat creation/ enhancement along the River.

Source: Hereford City Council BS7750 Review 1992

IBM have a track record of commitment to environmental excellence going back many years. However, they still felt it was appropriate to commission an external third-party report to review the progress made and to identify if there were any other areas for improvement. The resulting SustainAbility review, published in 1992, took a broad view across the organisation and made a number of recommendations for the further enhancement of environmental management. As you can see from the extract, some have already been addressed.

Recommendation 1:

In selecting the new Chairman for its Environment Council, IBM UK should consider selecting an individual closely identified with *mainstream* business requirements. The appointment will send important signals both inside and outside the company.

[Subsequent IBM UK actions: John Gillett appointed Chairman of the UK Environmental Operations Council and Ian Reynolds assumed Main Board responsibilities for the environment, together with the chairmanship of the UK Environmental Strategy Council.]

Source: IBM Environmental Review 1992.

CHECKLIST

- *Have you a clear scope for the review?*

- *Have the team participated fully in the programme design?*
- *Have you addressed the key issues?*
  - *Corporate and Business issues*: policy; practices; procedures; training; environmental auditing; environmental labelling; employees; banks; insurance; shareholders; transport; regulations.
  - *Operational issues*: health and safety; acoustics; COSHH; accidents; incidents; emergency plans.
  - *Environmental issues*: air (CO_2; global warming; pollutants; CFCs; Halon; acid rain); Water (supply quantity; supply quality; effluent discharges; conservation); waste (reduction; reuse; recycling; packaging; paper; minimisation); energy (power; lighting; fuels; efficiency); nature (resources use; raw materials; habitats; site management).
- *Does the SWOT analysis address all the management issues?*
- *Does the report identify highlights as well as problems and deficiencies?*
- *Does the report identify the resources and outline programme for implementation?*

COMMUNICATION HINTS

- Try to be as open and informative as possible on the exercise. You will want to share this information with the staff in the organisation when you introduce the awareness issue so try to let them know what's coming and when.

- Be specific about the source of the requirement, e.g. EPA1990 Schedule 1 and Schedule 2.
- Remember to build on existing practice, e.g. COSHH. You are not trying to re-invent the wheel.
- Use a variety of information gathering techniques, there are all types and styles of user out there, some like the interview, others the questionnaire. Asking the question in a range of ways, improves your response.
- Provide an executive summary in the report for those who are too busy to read the whole report. The summary should include: the policy development plan; an immediate action plan; and the EMS project management plan.

8

The environmental policy statement

The policy is not just in place as a public relations exercise; it is in place as a basis for developing more specific environmental objectives and targets throughout the different levels of the organisation: sites, functions, departments and individual job descriptions. The policy statement has to meet certain criteria to satisfy the requirements of BS7750 (see the checklist on page 78) including being published.

Because the application of the policy will result in changes in the way the organisation is managed, from the investment and strategic plans to the day-to-day operations, it must be owned and lead by the managers at the top of the organisation.

OBJECTIVE

The goal is an established environmental policy for the organisation.

Preparing a draft environmental policy statement

Building on the process for obtaining commitment discussed in chapter 5, we now follow the plan agreed in chapter 6. With the project team, review and agree the policy areas that were identified as a result of the preliminary review and prepare a draft environmental policy statement for the organisation.

Ask each member of the project team to review and obtain comment and approval from their managers. It is a line management issue and line management must have the opportunity to review and approve. After all, you want them to own the solutions they put in place, so it is important they are motivated to own those solutions by owning the problem statement.

Consolidate the feedback you get from the task force. You may be asked to make some changes. Consider them on their merits and discuss them if you are not clear about the concerns. Accept, modify or reject the proposed changes, but acknowledge and inform the commentators what you have done. With that agreement you are now in a position to go to the executive team.

Gaining the approval of senior management

You will need a 'slot' on the next meeting agenda. This will be in the plan so should be no surprise to anyone. Send the task force-approved draft to the executive team members ahead of the meeting. Your presentation then can be crisp and precise. It should:

- position the policy statement in the overall programme;
- state the requirements that the policy must meet;
- check they have read it!;
- present the policy, and expand and explain with examples the possible implications at each level;
- explain how they can measure attainment of the policy.

You must also listen to the responses and document any changes or qualifications. You can use a flip chart to write-up any changes in wording to get it agreed at that time. Remember that the policy statement is the key to the whole system, so although it will be subject to change and fine-tuning, it has to be as 'right' as it can be. When you have consensus, stop. Review both the internal and external communication plans in the light of the current consensus.

Immediately after the meeting, e.g. within twenty-four hours, send the agreed final wording to the executive for confirmation so that there are no errors or omissions. Confirm you are implementing the agreed communication plan.

Example

The Pilkington environmental policy statement (Fig. 8.1) shows an example of a corporate environmental policy.

PGL ENVIRONMENTAL POLICY

Our aim is profitable continuity. The core businesses provide flat and safety products for architectural and automotive markets. These products make an important contribution to improving living standards, to people's safety, to the conservation of energy, and are ecologically friendly.

We strive for the highest standards in all our operations, motivated by an acute awareness of the best international practices. We integrate environmental considerations in our business decision-making. We have an overriding commitment to the market, and sensitivity to the needs and interests of our customers.

To sustain and protect the environment, we will:

- conduct environmental audits of all our operations to ensure that waste and pollution is minimised.
- regulate and improve our manufacturing processes to cause the least practicable impact on the environment, encouraging our employees to help and investing ahead of legislative requirements.
- develop and market products that have excellent environmental characteristics and which meet the highest demands for efficiency.
- liaise with suppliers and customers to facilitate the best possible environmental practices in the manufacturing and installation chain, and promote the recycling of glass and related materials.
- co-operate with the appropriate authorities and technical organisations in the formation of standards and the means of compliance.
- promote and undertake educational programmes and discussion on Green issues for employees, suppliers, customers, schools and the community at large, protecting health and safety.
- discuss environmental issues regularly at the highest levels of the Company, and take a lead in Group initiatives.

Re-Confirmed by the
Pilkington Glass Limited Board
18th July, 1990

Rodney Stansfield

Rodney Stansfield, Chief Executive

Fig. 8.1 Extract from Pilkington's environmental policy statement
Source: Pilkington Group.

Designing the environmental awareness presentation

The results of the work done to date will provide the material for the awareness presentation. The objective is to raise the level of understanding in the organisation and activities due to take place.

It should be designed to be used as a self-contained package by yourself, members of the project team, departmental environmental co-ordinators or line managers themselves, depending on the type of organisation and skills available.

The presentation should be short, taking up to 40 minutes and be used within a management meeting agenda. It will introduce the audience to the environmental influences and potential pressures on the organisation that will result in some form of follow-up action by management to implement change.

The presentation will cover the following:

- The environmental issue generally
  - legislation press reports, other companies' actions;
- the pressures relevant to the company or business
  - industry specific issues, future legislation;
- the company response
  - the project outline, scope, resources and timetable, objectives and measurement;
- the preliminary review results
  - strengths, weaknesses, opportunities and threats;
- the organisation's environmental policy;
- the next steps in the programme.

In identifying the roles and responsibilities of various team members, highlight the need for a nominated environmental co-ordinator at departmental level. Allow the audience to consider how such a role might be filled and who might be most appropriate.

The presentation should conclude with some time for questions and answers, keeping notes of any issues raised that may need resolution after the conclusion of the presentation.

CHECKLIST

- *Does your environmental policy statement meet the criteria?*
- *Is it relevant?*
  The policy must relate to the activities of the organisation, the things produced and the effects identified in the preliminary review. Check back to the review conclusions.
- *Is it understood?*
  Check that all the managers are familiar with the policy throughout the organisation. Have the team members disseminated the policy to all their employees?
- *Can it be effective?*
  Check that the policy can be met by the organisation. Can it be turned into actions and measured?
- *Is it public?*
  Check that the procedure to publish the policy is effective.

- *Does it include a commitment to improvement?*
  Check that the improvement element is understood and is accepted.
- *Is it consistent?*
  Check that there is no conflict with other policy statements, e.g. the policy statements on Health and safety or quality.
- *Does it cover the key environmental impacts?*
  The policy statement must be comprehensive. Make sure it includes all the environmental impacts of your company, e.g. energy use, waste minimisation, resource use; pollution risks from plant and processes; upstream and downstream activities; projects and strategic plans.

Communicating the environmental policy statement to the workforce

Tell the managers first. Check that they have all they need to advise staff of the new policy. Give them some time to go back to their task force representative and agree any clarifications before releasing the policy more widely. Then tell everyone clearly and precisely. It is awareness and not action you are looking for, so keep it simple, and place it in context of the overall EMS programme.

Use different media – newsletters, posters, internal mail. Remember that an audience receives information in many different ways so use them all. Measure the impact by a follow-up survey to ensure that the message has been received.

COMMUNICATION HINTS

The policy should not be a bland statement, e.g. 'To be environmentally friendly . . .'. It need not be a performance pledge, e.g. 'To reduce NO^x emissions by 10 per cent in the next 12 months'. It should be a broad statement of the intentions of the organisation in the area of environmental performance that can be used by all parts of the organisation to develop their own targets in relation to the policy.

9

The implementation workshop

In setting up the original plan we identified two types of cascade. We have already seen how the *awareness presentation* can be used in communicating the environmental issue generally, introducing the policy statement, the environment project team, the commitment to achieving compliance to BS7750 and the Eco-management and audit Regulation. The *implementation workshop* is the main tool used in integrating the environmental management system into the business systems.

In large organisations the workshop will be one of many cascaded from the top of the organisation to the operations departments, in a small organisation there may be just one workshop. However, implementation workshops usually function on a departmental level, with a manager and his direct reporting staff.

OBJECTIVE

The goal is to achieve a draft environmental management system for each department of your company.

Setting up the agenda

The workshop is a form of meeting, so like all meetings it must have a specific purpose. An agenda, Example 9.1, should be designed to take you there. It should include the following aspects.

INTRODUCTION

As the programme manager you are responsible for introducing the workshop. You are there as the facilitator to enable the team to make progress.

Example 9.1

ENVIRONMENTAL MANAGEMENT SYSTEM PROGRAMME:
IMPLEMENTATION WORKSHOP AGENDA

- Introduction
- Objective
- Knowledge base
- Drivers for change
- The organisation's current status
- Environmental management standards
- Applied standards
- Action plan
- Knowledge review
- Workshop assessment

OBJECTIVES

The programme manager establishes the objectives for the workshop, so that the participants will know what the goal is and when you have succeeded. A suggested set of objectives is shown in Example 9.2. These can be varied but should not exceed three if the workshop is to be successful.

Example 9.2

ENVIRONMENTAL MANAGEMENT SYSTEM PROGRAMME:
IMPLEMENTATION WORKSHOP OBJECTIVES

At the end of this workshop you should have:

- An understanding of environmental issues in [name of company/department]
- An understanding of an environmental management system (EMS)
- An understanding of the process for implementing a documented EMS in [name of company/department]

KNOWLEDGE BASE

This is a simple element that has two functions: (a) to get your audience thinking and interested (it is important in interactive workshops that you facilite knowledge assimilation by the participants – do not try to force information into unwilling participants); and (b) to demonstrate that some knowledge has been gained after the workshop (an important reward for you and the participants). This part of the agenda should be fun. Example 9.3 demonstrates a 'quizz' technique for acquiring knowledge on BS7750 and the Eco-Management and audit Regulation.

Example 9.3

ENVIRONMENTAL MANAGEMENT SYSTEM PROGRAMME:
IMPLEMENTATION WORKSHOP KNOWLEDGE BASE

Answer *True*, *False* or *Don't Know* to the following statements and questions.

1. BS7750 is a mandatory British standard.
2. Compliance with the proposed EC Eco audit Regulation is mandatory for some industries.
3. Are parts of [name of company] certified to BS7750 by an accredited assessor?
4. It is a requirement of some of our customers that we comply with BS7750.
5. Non-compliance with BS7750 can be a breach of contract.
6. In order to comply with BS7750 and the Eco-Management and audit Regulation you must achieve zero emissions.
7. In order to comply with BS7750 you must continuously improve your environmental performance.
8. In order to comply with the Eco-Management and audit Regulation you must continuously improve your environmental performance.
9. Compliance with BS7750 confirms your legal compliance.
10. Assessment to BS7750 is just an extension of BS5750.

Ask them to put the questionnaire to one side for now.

DRIVERS FOR CHANGE

This takes the form of a guided discussion. Using one or two OHPs as a stimulus, ask questions of your audience to stimulate discussion and views from them. For example, 'What recent incidents or accidents have been reported in the news?' 'How might they affect us?'; 'What recent environmental legislation are they aware of?' 'What particular legal issues are relevant to us?'; 'What is meant by a Duty of Care?', etc.

Try to let the discussion move around the room by prompting for answers and providing information where needed. What you are looking for is the recognised desire to learn about this topic from the participants. A guideline for the discussion can be found in Example 9.4.

Example 9.4

ENVIRONMENTAL MANAGEMENT SYSTEM PROGRAMME:
IMPLEMENTATION WORKSHOP DRIVERS FOR CHANGE

- Legal issues — UK – EPA (Environmental Pollution Act)
  – Duty of Care
  Europe – EIA (environmental impact assessments)
  – CFCs
- Customers — Expectations and procurement policies
- Competitors — Actions, market growth and share
- Stakeholders — Banks, insurance, community, employees, suppliers, etc.
- Corporate — Programmes and policies
- Benefits — Energy and waste savings, cohension and motivation
- Marketing — New products and services

THE ORGANISATION'S CURRENT STATUS

With information from the preliminary review it should be possible to share with the workshop team as much as possible about the actual environmental performance of the organisation. Be factual and accurate. If you work in generalisations you will lose the audience.

Put the information across in a fun way. Get the audience to present parts of the data or provide some raw data and ask for an interpretation.

Try always to relate the issues back to the responsibilities of the participants. If they are in building or site services, focus on energy use, insulation and space efficiency. If they are marketing, focus on product performance, if in manufacturing, look at the use of resources and waste management factors.

ENVIRONMENTAL MANAGEMENT STANDARDS

This section is best done as a working exercise. Can you imagine being lectured to on the contents of a British Standard? Although a best seller and designed for easy comprehension, BS7750 still contains much 'standardese'. Anyway do you think your learners will learn if you just tell them?

So, we will ask the workshop participants to tell each other what they think the requirements mean. You can arbitrate any gross misunderstandings. Exercise 1 (see Example 9.5) is designed to challenge the participants to read, think about and tell others in the room how they understand the requirements and the implications on their current practices.

Example 9.5

ENVIRONMENTAL MANAGEMENT SYSTEM PROGRAMME:
IMPLEMENTATION WORKSHOP – EXERCISE 1

Review a specification clause or BS7750 and prepare a three-minute presentation to explain your understanding of the content.

APPLIED STANDARDS

This section provides an opportunity to explore with the workshop group how the standards might be applied in each participant's area of responsibility. Again, the best way to explore this is through an exercise (see exercise 2 in Example 9.6), not through your own or the manager's interpretation. This example uses eight headings to establish a 'skeleton' departmental EMS document.

Purpose	Strategy
Dependencies	Deliverables
Procedures	Measurements
Change Management	Improvement

Example 9.6

ENVIRONMENTAL MANAGEMENT SYSTEM PROGRAMME: IMPLEMENTATION WORKSHOP – EXERCISE 2

Review the following questions. Write down some notes under each heading. The results will be collated on flip-chart for the group.

Note: The elements of your business process have been divided up into eight parts for simplicity of analysis.

1. (a) *What is your main business purpose?*

   Mission/objectives/goal.

   (b) *What is your environmental policy relative to the mission?*

2. (a) *What is your strategy to achieve the main business purpose?*

   Input/major activities/outputs/roles and responsibilities/flow chart.

   (b) *Within this strategy what are the activities for implementing the environmental policy?*

3. (a) *What are you dependent on if you are to achieve your mission?*

   CSFs/customers/suppliers/staff/skills/job descriptions.

   (b) *Within those dependencies what are the significant environmental criteria?*

4. (a) *What must you deliver to meet the requirements of your mission?*

   Outputs/contracts/documents of understanding/service level agreements/performance plans.

   (b) *Within those deliverables what are the potential objectives and targets for environmental performance?*

5. (a) *What are the main procedures in implementing the strategy?*

   Operating instructions/process guides/schedules/checkpoints/detailed flow charts.

   (b) *What changes will be made to achieve the environmental performance objectives and targets?*

6. (a) *What do you measure to ensure the process is working effectively?*

Process measurements/key indicators/statistical quality control/self-assessments/reports/meetings.

(b) *Within these management controls how should environmental objectives and targets be measured?*

7. (a) *How do you manage change in the process?*

Requirements change control/error correction procedures/corrective action/document control/communications.

(b) *Within these procedures how would you manage environmental performance change requirements?*

8. (a) *How do you manage process improvement?*

Customer satisfaction/best-of-breed comparisons/process simplification/work elimination/cycle time reduction/productivity improvements.

(b) *Within these improvement procedures how would you manage environmental improvement?*

Each of the participants should have some notes on the questions. Draw up a flip chart and under each question go to a participant and capture his or her thoughts. Then check with the rest of the group that you have covered all the points. Hopefully the variety of thinking will result in additional contributions from all the participants.

The flip chart is now a valuable document! On it is captured the main business activities of the department or function, and the views of the manager and staff of the main environmental elements to be added to the management system. This chart provides data for:

(a) the departmental environmental management manual; and
(b) the action plan of environmental performance improvement.

ACTION PLAN

This part of the workshop is your opportunity to obtain the agreements of those present to proceed towards a programme of improvement in their area. They now have it all:

- They know the problem or challenge exists; they even know they don't know all the answers.

- They know the standards to be attained.
- They know where they will start to look at implementing change, within their own activities.

Now you need to ascertain the key activities. Do not forget that for each action you must ascribe ownership, set a date by which the action is to be complete, and establish a measurement by which you will all know it has been completed.

KNOWLEDGE REVIEW

Having agreed the action plan, now is the time to review the knowledge questionnaire – some notes may help you with anything not already clear.

1. Compliance with BS7750 is voluntary.
2. Participation in Eco-Management and audit regulation is voluntary, it is aimed at certain industry sectors defined in the Regulation.
3. There is no *accredited* certification available in the UK at this time.
4. Compliance with BS7750 may be required by some purchasers in the future.
5. If compliance with BS7750 was a contract condition, not complying would be a breach of contract.
6. There is no requirement for zero-emissions.
7. BS7750 requires *continual* improvement in performance.
8. The Eco-Management and audit regulation requires continuous improvement.
9. BS7750 does not confirm legal compliance. It may help you understand where you are, and what corrective action to take.
10. The requirements for BS7750 include activities not addressed in BS5750, although the two are designed to be complementary.

Some of these points will encourage further discussion and clarification of the meaning and intent, it is not competition!

WORKSHOP ASSESSMENT

The workshop is key to implementing the programme, therefore you need to know if it has been successful, and if you have a number to run, any improvements that can be made.

A simple assessment sheet will provide you with feedback on the success of the workshop, assessing the audience satisfaction in three areas; met objectives; presentation content; presentation style.

EMS IMPLEMENTATION WORKSHOP – ASSESSMENT

1. How satisfied are you that the workshop met its objections?
   Very satisfied satisfied neutral dissatisfied v. dissatisfied
2. How satisifed are you with the presentation materials?
   Very satisfied satisfied neutral dissatisfied v. dissatisfied
3. How satisfied are you with the presentation style?
   Very satisfied satisfied neutral dissatisfied v. dissatisfied

Have you any suggestions for improving the workshop?

Ascribing a score for each response will allow you to evaluate the workshop's success in achieving the objectives.

CHECKLIST FOR ACTION

- *Do the actions establish realistic and meaningful improvements.*
- *Can the actions be quantified?*
- *Are there areas where more information is needed to establish objectives and targets?*
- *Check with the superior department or function to see if they are properly aligned.*
- *Check with preliminary review considerations.*

What next?

Having completed the workshop, document the discussion and outcome, the action plan and dates for future reviews. Ensure that this information is shared both up and down the management line, and to all related departments, suppliers and customers. Remember this will result in some changes in those relationships. The best way to ensure that the change is accepted, is to share the thought process behind them. Emphasise that this is not revolution but evolution. It does not supersede or replace the core business needs and demands. It is not another management system.

COMMUNICATION HINTS: FACILITATION

Facilitation is not training under another name, it is a conscious attempt to focus the learning experience on the learner. To do this you need to think from the learner's perspective.

- What does the learner need to know and why?
- What are the benefits from learning?
- How can the learner be stimulated to learn?
- What fun can be had in learning?

This last one is essential. The learning experience is one divorced from the day-to-day issues of the workplace where to take a risk and fail is bad. So people do not do it. In a workshop, however, you can encourage risk taking and making mistakes because it doesn't really matter. It can be fun to fail and you learn so much more.

In designing workshops like these, remember the intention is to help the participants 'grow' *their* knowledge, not give you an opportunity to demonstrate yours. The acronym, GROW, is useful in this context.

G – goals
R – reality
O – options
W – wrap-up

Goals – establish what you want to achieve and provide a test to know when you will have succeeded. Prioritise the goals to a limited number that are achievable.
Reality – identify the perceived problem, what the symptoms are, what the inhibitors or constraints to resolving the problem are, and what the potential enablers to achieve success are. Do you need more information? What should the solution look like? Establish your criteria.
Options – open up solutions, choices and directions. Test them against the criteria, and model the possibilities or instigate a trial.
Wrap-up – implement the agreed direction, follow-up the action plan, and track and measure against the agreed action plan.

10

Establishing management responsibilities and resources

This chapter is about establishing the necessary management authority, organisation, skills and resources to deliver the environmental policy. The requirements of the plan will commit you to the involvement of all the managers and staff throughout the organisation. You must define the roles and responsibilities for *all* those who manage or perform work that affects the environment. That is just about everyone!

To ensure that you have all the roles, responsibilities, authority and interrelationships defined you must have a *documentation mechanism*. You will already have some form of organisation chart from the highest level down to the job descriptions and performance plans at the individual level. The intention is not to re-invent the wheel, just make effective use of the processes you have in place. If you are going to take your managers and staff with you, it is much easier to build on an existing foundation than to start from scratch when your peers are not sure what kind of new structure you have in mind. The end result should be an extension to the management system that ensures that all managers and staff have an environmental objective in their individual job descriptions and performance measurements. If your organisation pays on performance, then such an integrated approach will ensure that the environmental performance issue has the correct balance in the organisation's activities.

Each manager must be able to act in a way appropriate to the responsibilities that are relevant to his or her area of environmental performance. The integration of each functional and departmental manager within the overall policy is the role of the management representative. Together the network of integrated responsibilities must be adequate to implement the system. A management representative should be appointed whose responsibility is to ensure that the requirements of the Standard are met.

In order to know if the system is designed and operating effectively you will need to verify compliance. There is therefore a need to provide adequate resources to verify performance. Verification is the process of checking or testing to ensure that a process, practice or procedure complies with the requirements. In the EMS this includes the activities to assure compliance with the Standard, through self-assessment, audit and review.

OBJECTIVE

The goal is to establish a set of management responsibilities and resources sufficient to implement and support the environmental management system.

Roles and responsibilities

The key to establishing the network of management responsibilities is the elements of the implementation workshop that identify the roles and responsibilities (strategy), set job descriptions (dependencies) and performance plans (deliverables). Integrating the environmental policy and performance standards into these categories will provide the matrix of authority necessary to achieve the goal. A departmental organisation should be established to ensure that each key activity is clearly identified as belonging to a specific job holder. The allocation of activities to job holders should be outlined in a *job description*, which will define the outputs for which the job holder is responsible. This is important because given the organisational changes that frequently occur in companies, a continuity of staff functions is essential if environmental performance to the BS7750 standards is to be maintained. When jobs are actually changed and the organisation expands or slims down, it is important to know all the responsibilities that are being affected. It is often easy to overlook infrequent activities in a time of change – an oversight which can have significant repercussions.

JOB DESCRIPTIONS

Define roles in the company in such a way that the job holder, and others with whom the job holder interacts, has a clear understanding of the responsibilities and authority which enables him or her to act. It puts a boundary around the job. The job description must specify the performance criteria deemed necessary to complete the task, e.g. the performance criteria for a typist might be the ability to type 60 words per minute.

The most important factor in job description is the balance between responsibility and authority: responsibility for certain tasks must be supported with the resources to complete the task and the authority to act if the task is to be completed. For example, if you identify that a job holder is responsible for providing an emergency response service to tanker drivers, indicate the performance criteria for a given response time and ensure that the resources and authority to use those resources are made available to that individual.

Job descriptions usually have two elements: a general description of the role and responsibilities and an element of performance management. The performance part of the job description will expand on responsibilities part. It should set out the achievements that are required if the job holder is to meet his or her key responsibilities and major goals. For example, within a departmental function, let's say 'site facilities management', the role of energy management may be delegated to one member of staff. The job description should provide the boundaries of the individual's activities. If the description requires that bills are to be *paid* on time, then that is what the individual should do. If, however, the intention is to *manage* energy use, then the job description should reflect that. The description may therefore include an analysis of energy use; and propose changes to tariffs, equipment, installations, practices and procedures in order to achieve better energy use and efficiency. Job descriptions form a major element of the EMS documentation.

Within the job description and responsibilities must lie clarification of authority for the acting in emergency situations. Detailed descriptions of emergency procedures will be documented in the emergency plan, it is ownership of the documentation and emergency response that must be ascribed in the job descriptions. This includes the authority to act and commit resources in emergency situations.

PERFORMANCE PLANNING

Performance planning translates general roles and responsibilities into specific and observable end results or 'outputs'. Most job descriptions list a range of responsibilities which result in between six and nine outputs – any more and it becomes difficult to prioritise the roles. For every output there will need to be some measurement or indicator to determine the quality of the output. Does it meet the specified requirements? Only then can the individual be appropriately assessed. The performance plan should indicate the outputs and the performance criteria against which the assessment will be made (see Table 10.1). Sometimes the performance plan may include reference to some of the activities to be undertaken in achieving the objectives.

Table 10.1

Objectives	*Performance criteria*	*Assessment*
Output: To reduce energy demand and costs on the [site name] site by 5 per cent over 1992 (assumes constant demand)	*Indicators* ■ Achievement against budget ■ Impact on business ■ Investment payback criteria met ■ Quarterly control reports ■ Supplier relationships	

Establishing resources

From the implementation workshop you have gained an understanding of the dependencies to achieve the desired environmental performance standard. These resources include people with dedicated responsibilities to support the programme of work, e.g. environmental programme managers, departmental co-ordinators and EMS auditors; some equipment and systems support needed to establish the integrated EMS network in a co-ordinated manner across the business; some financial resources to support specific areas of technical expertise e.g. consultants; some financial resources to procure equipment or tests to support the operational control activities at technical level.

Resources will need to be identified in every function, department and level balanced to meet the needs of that particular area in achieving its environmental performance goals. You will need to ensure that each departmental co-ordinator reviews the need for resources in a timely way, through regular reviews in the project team meetings.

Establishing verification methods

The requirements for verification include the necessary protocols and procedures for auditing the environmental management system, together with appropriately trained personnel.

You will need to document the proposed EMS audit plans and protocols, (see chapter 18) and include reference to this documentation in the EMS manual, (see chapter 15).

The audit staff will need to have a range of skills in:

- *Leading audit programmes* The lead auditor will require experience in audit practice and procedure, project management and interpersonal skills. A thorough knowledge of ISO10,011: Quality systems auditing, and BS7750 is required.
- *Auditors* In support of the lead auditor, the team will need familiarity with systems auditing and good interpersonal skills, a thorough knowledge of BS7750. Specialist auditor skills may be needed in
  – Industry specific: where the organisation faces specific issues it may be necessary to ensure the resources include relevant expertise e.g. steel, oil or chemical production process knowledge.
  – Environmental specific: where the organisation faces particular environmental performance problems, it may be necessary to ensure the resources include relevant expertise: e.g. environmental pollution monitoring, waste minimisation techniques or emission control.

The management representative

The management representative is a senior manager, usually on the executive board, with specific responsibilities of overseeing the implementation of the programme. It is usual to appoint an operations manager to implement the programme, reporting to the management representative.

The role involves working with peer executives to ensure the commitment to the goal is consistently applied, overseeing the progress to plan and representing the organisation externally.

Integration of roles and responsibilities

It is important to review the roles and responsibilities of personnel with defined authority to ensure that there are no gaps, which might lead to errors or omissions, or overlaps, which might lead to duplication of effort and resources.

In order to achieve this integration there are a number of actions you can encourage:

- *service level agreements* – mini-contracts between departments to ensure co-operation in areas of mutual dependency;
- *co-ordination meetings* – regular cross-functional or departmental meetings to review areas of common concern or changes in practices and procedures;
- *central directory* – maintain a directory of process ownership, roles and responsibilities in the environmental management manual to ensure a complete matrix of responsibilities is available;
- *publish departmental representatives* – In the environmental management manual, house magazine or quality system, publicise the key contacts for activities and processes related to environmental performance issues.

Example

The Body Shop's definition of roles and responsibilities within the company is shown in Fig. 10.1. It shows the links between the central environmental departmental and the rest of the management structure. This ranges from interest at the board to individual shop environmental advisers (SEAs) which take responsibility for environmental activities in the shop – energy monitoring, recycling programmes and waste management, etc.

An example from IBM (Fig. 10.2) illustrates the main functions of the environmental affairs organisation in the UK. From the UK management board setting policies, to the operating unit responsibility for performance measurements.

CHECKLIST

- *Have all the departmental staff got documented job descriptions?*
- *Does the job description cover:*
  - *staff and resources adequate to achieve the objectives?*
  - *clear descriptions of authority to act?*
  - *clear responsibility for investigation and documentation?*
  - *clear authority to take action to solve problems?*
- *Have you identified the requirements for verification activities?*
- *Have you identified the verification resources?*

EXTERNAL COLLABORATION

THE BOARD
The policy-making and agenda setting forum. All Board members take a keen and active interest in our environmental performance and are kept fully up-to-date with what's going on by the Environmental Affairs General Manager.

GENERAL MANAGERS
There are twelve General Managers - including one for Environmental Affairs - who are responsible for the key operational and retailing areas. They meet monthly to discuss Company-wide issues.

SENIOR MANAGERS
They are responsible for individual departments. Those with operational responsibilities meet weekly at a meeting attended by the Environmental Affairs General Manager.

THE ENVIRONMENTAL CHARTER GROUP
A group of staff with a strong personal interest in environmental issues act as our environmental conscience. As such they are independent from the main environmental management system. They look at levels of environmental awareness among employees and make a quarterly award for excellence in environmental performance.

THE ENVIRONMENTAL DEPARTMENT
Four full-time staff and one full-time External Consultant are responsible for auditing as well as environmental research, policy development and campaigning. One person looks after Departmental Environmental Advisers, another looks after Shop Environmental Advisers and a new member of staff will be recruited this year to work with International Environmental Co-ordinators. The Department also has a Secretary who looks after all environmental documentation.

At the helm is the General Manager with overall responsibility for the environmental performance of the Company. The External Consultant looks after the development of Life Cycle Assessments for products and packaging and also liaises with our suppliers on environmental matters.

DEPARTMENTAL ENVIRONMENTAL ADVISERS
Each department nominates a highly dedicated person interested in environmental issues to play a part-time environmental role - a few hours each week. The 30 DEAs (some departments have more than one) meet monthly. Individually they also have close contact with the Environmental Department.

INTERNATIONAL ENVIRONMENTAL CO-ORDINATORS
Either employed or nominated by the International Head Franchise Operator in each country to be responsible for in-country environmental management. Sometimes this is a full-time appointment (often combined with a community projects role) but most co-ordinators are part-time. At the moment UK and International Franchise Operators are not directly linked into the environmental management system of the Company and there are no specific environmental measures built into the franchise agreement. In practice this is not a constraint as franchisees are selected on the basis of shared values and common aims.

UK SHOP ENVIRONMENTAL ADVISERS
Shop staff in non-management positions who take responsibility for the environmental management of their shop and for campaigning on a local level. So far there are nearly 200 SEAs who receive a minimum of one day's training and devote time each week to environmental issues.

TASK FORCES
Made up of operational and retailing staff, Task Forces meet to resolve cross-departmental environmental issues.

They will play an increasingly important role in developing and implementing policy (including the recommendations of this Statement).

Fig. 10.1 Roles and responsibilities within the Body Shop.
Source: The Green Book, Body Shop International, 1992

- *Have you assigned trained personnel?*
- *Have you appointed the management representative?*

COMMUNICATION HINTS

- Establish an award for managers, as well as staff, to win for significant contributions to the promotion of environmental performance improvement in any of the key functions.
- Establish a voluntary programme of workshops or committees to work on aspects of environmental improvement in the community around the organisations' sites.
- Contribute to local education and training establishments with presentation material and staff resources.

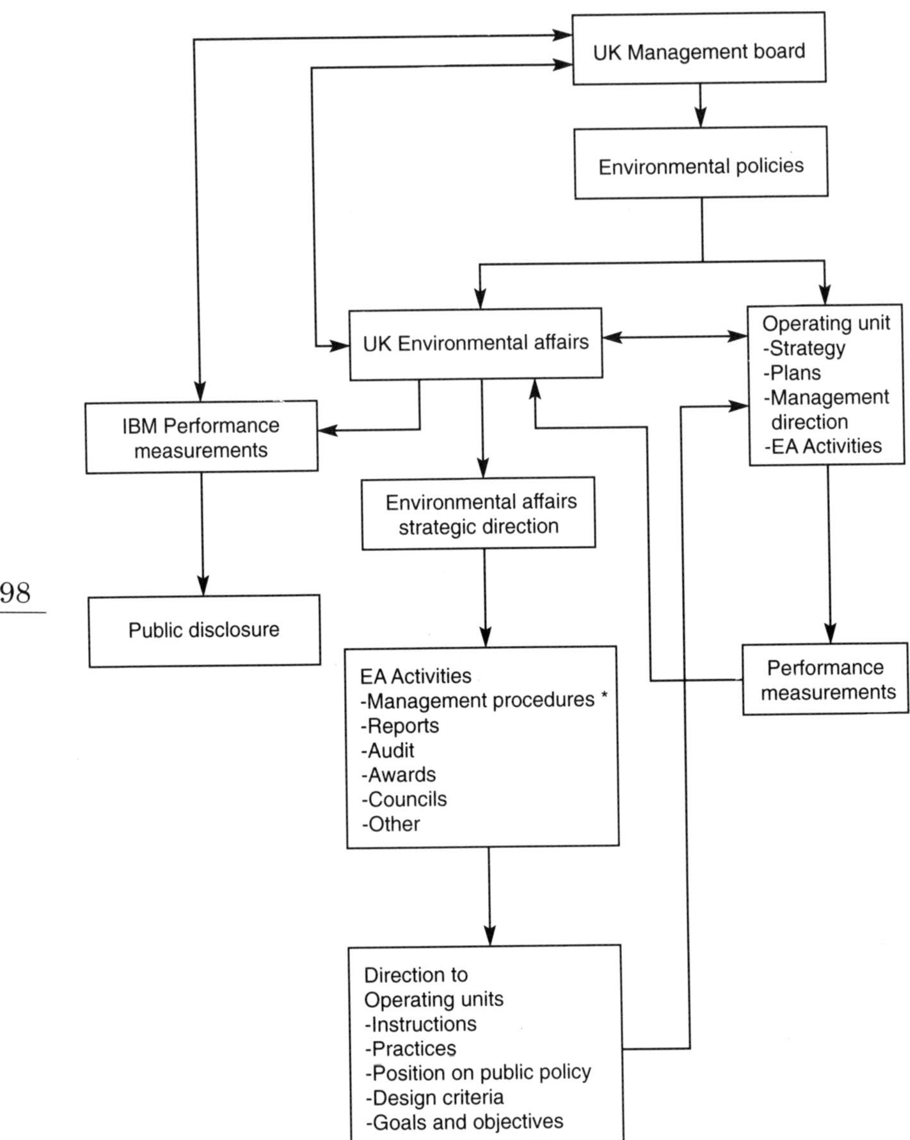

Fig. 10.2 The main functions of the environmental affairs organisation in the UK
Source: IBM

Communications and training

This chapter is about establishing the necessary communications, training plans, training records and integration to enable the environmental programme to be sufficiently understood and woven into the business so that environmental performance measurably improves. The programme must therefore be designed to ensure that managers and staff have access to the necessary education and training to enable them to fulfil their duties.

To communicate effectively you must know what you want to achieve as a result of the communication. If it is to let people know about an event, e.g. an opening of a new location or a new product launch, which may not require any action or response, it can be done by newsletter, management announcement or notice-board message. If you need to target a specific audience with information, you should address them directly. At the outset you must establish who the audience is and how best to contact them. If you wish your audience to *do* something about the information they receive, then you have to design the message and use the right medium to ensure you get the response you need.

OBJECTIVE

Your objective is to implement an effective communications programme and supporting training programme within your organisation.

Effective communications

There are three key components of effective communication:

- Know the desired response;
- Know the level of leadership interaction required; and
- Know the complexity of the information.

Figure 11.1 illustrates the interaction of the components. Leadership interaction is the extent to which managers involve themselves in supportive or directive behaviour with their staff. There is no 'best' leadership style, the balance depends on the maturity of the individual in the new role and the challenges being faced (see Fig. 11.2). Complexity of information is the extent to which the content of the message is readily understood.

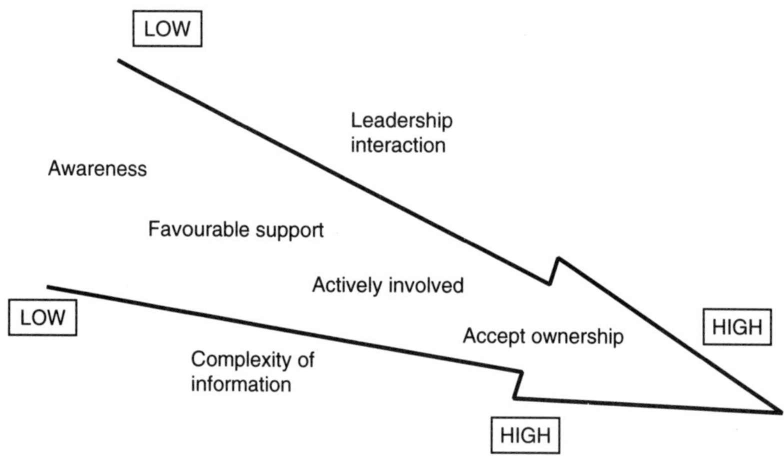

Fig. 11.1 Communications matrix

Leadership interaction in Fig. 11.2 suggests:

- *Directing* – low supportive behaviour with high directive behaviour – 'Please do it this way'
- *Coaching* – high supportive behaviour with high directive behaviour – 'Please do it this way, but before you do, let us discuss any points you have!'
- *Supporting* – low directive behaviour with high supporting behaviour – 'How do think we should do this?'
- *Delegating* – low directive behaviour and low supportive behaviour – 'Please deal with this!'

If the objective of the communication is merely to make staff aware of something the level of leadership interaction will be small, and the content of the message simple. However, if your communication requires

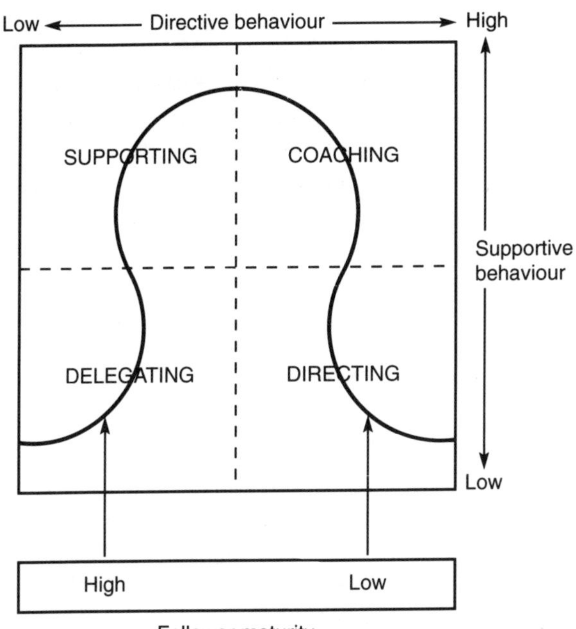

Fig. 11.2 ***Note*: Follower maturity and the situation will indicate the most appropriate leadership style**

Source: The One-minute Manager, Kenneth Blanchard, Donald Carew and Eunice Parisi-Carew, Fontana (an imprint of HarperCollins Publishers Limited), 1993.

action the level of leadership interaction will increase, as can the complexity of the message. The same is true in reverse. If you are not prepared to put the appropriate management time into a complex communication, you will not get the response you desire. Your communications plan, therefore, must be designed to balance the desired response with the necessary leadership interaction and complexity of information.

A further consideration, of course, is the capacity of the recipient to understand and implement the new information. To communicate effectively you must take into account the learning styles of the managers involved.

LEARNING STYLES

We all learn. However, as we move through life we find the process of learning changes. At school we are taught by others who know things we do not. Whether through discovery or by rote, we have information pushed at us. As adults we tend to learn what we want to learn or that which is presented in such a way that learning is easy and pleasurable. If we are not interested we have the capacity to 'switch off' and cease to learn.

An important factor in developing communications and training programmes is the learning styles of the intended recipients. In the same way that we are biased towards different aspects of activity – thinking (theorist), planning (pragmatist), doing (activist) or measuring (reflector), people have propensities to learn in different ways:

- *Theorists* – learn better when there is a conceptual approach to the subject.
- *Pragmatists* – understand that theory is all very well, but how can it be translated into reality? How would we plan to implement the idea?
- *Activists* – like to know what has to be done, and learn best by participating in the process.
- *Reflectors* – like to understand the anticipated results of the actions and measures the responses that are achieved.

We all possess a variety of these traits. Therefore, if communicators want their messages to be absorbed and acted upon, they must present the message in a combination of ways to cover the range of learning styles of the audience. The same technique must, of course, be used by trainers. In designing training support of the EMS implementation programme trainers must make the learning pleasurable and stimulating, and combine the different learning styles.

Obstacles to effective communication

In the light of the EMS implementation programme, the success of the communications system lies in the ability of the workforce to implement the organisational changes required to improve environmental standards. In order to encourage an active and participatory approach managers must consider the capacity of staff members to effect change. There is nothing more frustrating than to be encouraged to change the way we carry out our day-to-day activities, only to find that the changes we propose are inhibited by others in the organisation who do not appear to have the same message about the need for change. Those at the top of the organisation hold the key to making changes. Organisation hierarchies mean that often those who 'own' the business processes (i.e. senior managers) have less awareness of the impact and effectiveness of these processes than do the staff whose function is to make them work. If the management approach is *not* to encourage change, because to do so challenges the authority of the process owner, then ineffective processes often continue to operate even though the operators know they can be improved. The fear factor is at work. Table 11.1 shows how the management tiers usually operate within organisations.

Table 11.1 Management tiers with respect to process ownership and practice

	Process ownership	*Process practice*
Senior management	HIGH	LOW
Middle management	MIXED	MIXED
Operations staff	LOW	HIGH

The understanding of management tiers has led to the movement of empowerment in management training today. Empowerment encourages staff to make change happen and to accept their individual roles in making the processes work by contributing to the system design and taking ownership for the quality of work they see in front of them. For Nissan it means putting stop buttons on the production line and encouraging staff to use them if they see defective products going by. Empowerment means removing the 'fear factor' of being caught doing things wrong.

Business processes

Business processes are a series of linked activities that have a defined start point, from an input, proceed through a series of actions to an output with added value.

For example, paying a supplier invoice starts with the receipt of an invoice and goes through various checks to ensure validity of work done, validity of the value against an order and a check to ensure authority to pay is appropriate. The output, a payment to the supplier, follows.

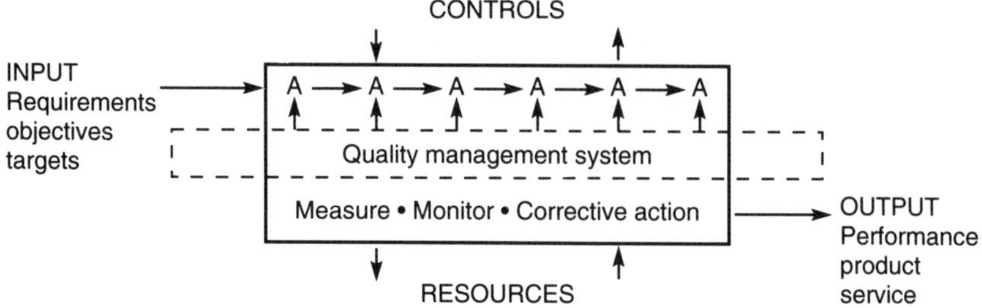

Business process
A series of linked actions from a defined start point (input) to a specific result (output)

The quality management system measures, monitors and controls the activities within the process. To ensure the output meets all requirements – customer, organisation & environment.

Fig. 11.3

104 The 'fear factor'

The root of the 'fear factor' is the fear of the unknown and it can seriously affect the change of any management system, including the EMS. It is essential to eradicate the 'fear factor' in change management if you are going to succeed in implementing your EMS programme. You want to encourage good performance from staff in areas which are unfamiliar to them. Your staff must gain confidence and knowledge in those areas. Reduce the fear of the unknown and the fear of failure at the outset and you are more likely to succeed in your objective. The fear of failure is the key – do away with this and people will respond to change enthusiastically.

You can reduce the 'fear factor' in many small ways at the lowest level in the process, but to allow that to happen you have to start at the top and displace the current paradigm of 'management knows best'. Managers have to start to see themselves as enablers, supporting the staff in implementing the goals and objectives set by managers. The manager is the person who removes inhibitors to progress, not creates or supports them. An education programme will go through a number of phases to achieve this: from awareness and consciousness, through understanding and agreement to implementation.

Implementing an education or training programme

Establishing an education and training programme is essential not only for educating your organisation's workforce about environmental standards, but also, and most importantly, for removing fears and easing through the change management strategies necessary for improving environmental performance. You will probably need to set up education and support programmes for your managers and operations staff alike. Workshops are an excellent example of a way of educating staff at various levels of the organisation. We have already examined awareness presentations and implementation workshops: the former improve *awareness*, *consciousness* and *understanding* while the latter help *resolve* problems through *agreement* and *implementation*. They are a particularly good way of educating your key EMS implementation personnel.

IDENTIFYING YOUR TRAINING NEEDS

The *skills analysis technique* is a useful tool in identifying your training needs. It establishes what kind of training is needed on an individual basis. In the development of your departmental EMS documentation you have incorporated detailed job descriptions of the key personnel of your implementation programme. Each job description can now be analysed to establish the range of skills required to implement the role satisfactorily. Ask your staff to indicate their individual levels of skills against the skills requirements of their specific job descriptions. Where the level of skills fails to match the skills requirement you have identified the training needs.

It is important to consider the different skills areas that are involved. These can be divided into two categories.

(a) Technical – the knowledge required to do the jobs; vocational or industry-specific knowledge.
(b) Personal – the interactive and personal skills that enhance ability to do the job.

You may also need to consider the specific skills required for implementing the EMS standards programme. For example, quality management techniques; process assessment analysis; audit and assessment activities; legislative knowledge; or environmental effects analysis procedures.

Having identified your training needs you now know what components your training programme must include.

Keeping training records

The various forms of internal training to ensure the skills gap is closed need to be recorded to ensure you have an appropriate audit trail, but also to ensure you know the extent of trained resources available to you.

To avoid an unwieldy system, training records should be kept in a single place, owned by the environmental programme manager, or training department. These can be individual records maintained in staff records, but you will still need a co-ordinating register to demonstrate that the range of skills required are available.

A model for a successful communications programme

You will know when you have succeeded in implementing an effective communications programme because your company will be well on its way to achieving the requirements of BS7750. The following model illustrates how an integrated communications programme, as part of your EMS, takes the company along from unconscious incompetence to unconscious competence – the ultimate objective of any effective management system.

UNCONSCIOUS INCOMPETENCE

Staff are unaware of the environmental issues and the present management system's shortcomings. New issues are being introduced although staff are unaware that anything is wrong or that there are other, better, ways of doing things – either to achieve the same standards more effectively and with less resources, or to achieve higher standards with similar effort through continual improvement.

Communications at this stage start at a low interaction/complexity level to raise awareness of the environmental issues. 'I understand that there are global environmental problems. Other organisations understand and are changing their responses. We will be considering our position and responding to these issues.

The initial communications programme and awareness presentation will have done this with the information received from the preliminary review which has highlighted areas of performance standards that fall short of the best practice or desired direction. A review of the draft organisational environmental policy and its potential impact on the department, together with a look at the anticipated programme for the next steps in the communication programme will indicate where communications should be focused.

It is important to measure the penetration of the information flow and the understanding that is achieved. It is difficult to move on to the next stage unless you have agreement at this one. Repeat the awareness programme if understanding of the issues is less than 50 per cent satisfaction.

CONSCIOUS INCOMPETENCE

Staff are aware of the issues and some of the system failures, strengths, weaknesses, opportunities and threats. There is a consciousness of the issues at a global and a local level and some immediate changes may be proposed by action-oriented staff.

Communications at this stage are high in interaction/complexity and aim to achieve commitment to the issues and make changes to achieve the new goals. 'My function/department has a role to play in support of the organisation's overall business goals. In doing so we have these environmental effects, can manage them better, and this is what we are going to do. . . .'

The follow-up implementation workshop will do this with a detailed study of the department operations and existing management systems, identification of the environmental effects, objectives and targets, and programmes for implementation. A number of actions will arise that will initiate the gathering of more information, the commencement of initiatives or projects and the building of teams to address the issues. At this stage, if it is well done, there will be a demand for more information on process analysis, effects analysis, statistics and improvements in project management. You must ensure that there is an appropriate level of expertise to respond and maintain momentum.

CONSCIOUS COMPETENCE

Having made changes to processes and systems to achieve higher standards of performance, staff are now aware of the benefits and improvements in performance standards. At this stage they are sustained because they *know* that they are doing things in a better way.

Communications at this stage focus on the inward recording and reinforcing of achievements and support to the changes. 'I understand the environmental policy and targets and the role I and my department can play in contributing to the organisation and global environmental issues. We are doing things differently now and I can show you what and how.' Communications activities are focused on recognition, reward and highlighting the changes.

UNCONSCIOUS COMPETENCE

Staff are now unaware of the automatic management processes now in place to establish and maintain performance to high environmental standards in all existing or new activities.

Communications focus on business-as-usual reporting and measurement but include all the new and evolving environmental criteria. Staff are now more outward facing, ensuring that full benefits are obtained from the investment, and involving and developing partnership with customers, suppliers and the community. 'I include environmental standard issues in my day-to-day business management systems. I can help you improve your environmental standards performance, so let's discuss how, and the mutual benefits.' However, although communications are now back to business-as-usual, they are monitored to ensure that the correct balance is retained in reporting the successes and benefits flowing from the programme implementation. Staff and managers, as a matter of course, take ownership and responsibility for implementing change in the organisation at every level.

CHECKLIST

- *Have you established a communication programme that:*
  - *Is relevant to the message – information or involvement?*
  - *Is supported by the right amount of leadership interaction?*
  - *Is designed to appeal to all the learning styles in the audience?*

- *Have you established a training programme that:*
  - *Analyses the skills needs relevant to the new requirements?*
  - *Assesses the skill mix currently available.*
  - *Identifies the skill gaps for training?*
- *Have you established an effective training records system:*
  - *Available at a central point?*
  - *Owned and maintined by a specified jobholder?*
- *Does the training content ensure awareness of:*
  - *Importance of compliance with environmental policy and objectives?*
  - *Potential environmental effects of their work activities?*
  - *Roles and responsibilities in relation to environmental performance management?*
  - *Risks in non-compliance with environmental performance standards?*

12

Environmental effects

BS7750 uses the term 'environmental effects' rather than the more familiar 'environmental impacts', or the less known but useful 'environmental burden'. 'Effects' is used because it covers the positive as well as the negative aspects of an organisation's environmental performance. Recognising the positive aspects can be just as beneficial to improving environmental performance as correcting the negative aspects. Companies must document and communicate their effects on the environment, both positive and negative, direct and indirect, not only to be able to set environmental targets and objectives, but also to demonstrate to assessors that the requirements of BS7750 are being met.

OBJECTIVE

The goal is to establish and maintain procedures for analysing and documenting the environmental effects of your company and communicating these effects to relevant interested parties.

The register of legislative, regulatory and other policy requirements

Your company must meet the law. You must therefore have mechanisms within the management system to ensure that legislative, regulatory and other policy requirements (e.g. corporate practices or industry-specific guidelines) are known, documented and monitored in your company. This allows you to feel confident about legal compliance and to audit that compliance.

Organisations may use many routes in compiling their registers. Some use professionals, for example external legal advisers (your company solicitor), internal legal advisers (your company secretary), or technical experts with specific areas of legal knowledge (safety managers). Others use a combination of internal professional skills and support documentation. Publications like *Croners* or *Barbour Index* provides a comprehensive database that is current and automatically updated with the latest environmental regulations. You may employ professional staff and then encourage participation in continuous professional development (CDP) training courses to keep the knowledge current. Most professional bodies now require some form of CPD.

Two factors come together at this point:

1. The preliminary review results which will have provided some basic information about the activities, legal issues and stakeholder issues you face.

2. The output from the implementation workshops at every functional/ departmental level in the organisation. Output from the workshop included a response to the skeleton EMS which required consideration of the key documentation and the 'deliverables' in terms of environmental performance.

Documentation requirements will be different in the various parts of the organisation, depending on the criticality of legal and regulatory affairs in relation to the activities and processes involved. For example, the machine shop will have very different legislative considerations from the site services department or the transport department. The levels of knowledge required by staff and management will also be significantly different. Documentation procedures will therefore need to be department-specific to be effective. Registers can be consistent in presentation across the organisation but designed on a departmental basis. In addition to listing the legislative, regulatory and other policy requirements relevant to the department, the registers should

- specify ownership of the documentation;
- indicate who has access to the information;
- identify a system of measurement or assessment;
- specify when the information is to be received, updated, etc.

THE LEGISLATIVE, REGULATORY AND POLICY REQUIREMENTS

This part of the register must be comprehensive. Assess existing company records, focusing on waste management practices, raw materials supplies, etc; examine key business processes and safety requirements; incorporate the local authority's requirements for control of accidents and emergencies; include consents for discharges, licences to treat or dispose of waste, duty of care procedures, APC and EPA consents, and other requirements of current legislation. All the legislative requirements relevant to your industry? For example:

- Planning – requirements or restraints included in planning consents
- Safety – Health and Safety at Work Act (HASAWA), COSHH, fire precautions and safe working practices
- Consents – discharge and extraction authorisations National Rivers Authority (NRA)
- IPC – scheduled process authorisations
- Protocols – Montreal protocol on CFCs
- Asbestos – location registers
- Corporate – energy plans, environmental master plans.

OWNERSHIP

The register must specify who in the organisation is responsible for keeping the documentation current and in place. The responsibility goes with the position, not the individual, who may move on to another job within the organisation. For example, the fire certificate might be the responsibility of the Site Services Manager, or the discharge consents the responsibility of the Process Engineer.

ACCESSIBILITY

The register must indicate who needs to have access to the information for action and measurement. It may be just the individual who holds the data (as with the fire certificate), or it may be that, in order to ensure that the discharge consent is met, many more people on the shop floor need to know about permits and measures of compliance.

Other aspects of the legal requirement may require an 'indirect' knowledge level. For example, HASAWA regulations require safe systems of work for the entire workforce. Not everyone needs to know the detailed requirements, but all must have access to the safe systems of work information, whether inside or outside the company, and all contractors coming on to sites need to know about safety procedures, permits to work, access arrangements to confined spaces, etc.

MEASUREMENT SYSTEMS

The register must identify the key documentation that should be present and in order to measure your company's compliance to the requirements you have set out. Your audits should regularly assess the extent, currency and accessibility of the legislative and regulatory registers.

DATES

The register must specify when the data are due for review, updating or replacing if out of date. Your register needs to look forward to planned legislation as well as current requirements. When planning the future performance targets of your organisation, it is essential that you consider forthcoming legislative requirements so that new product development, for example, can take into account the possible implications of new legislation and net waste investment. It would be inappropriate to design a process to current legislative requirements, knowing that the criteria for compliance are likely to change.

In addition, because requirements change and legislative demands are becoming more stringent, you will find a need to retain some historic data. The environmental effects of past activities can have significant consequences. At some time in the future, it may be essential to be able to demonstrate that, at the time of the discharge or event, you were operating within relevant legislation.

Example

Figure 12.1 is an extract from Hereford City Council's Register of Regulations (June 1992) which shows the discharges to sewer relevant regulations for consideration.

Discharges to Sewer

Hereford has consent to discharge trade effluents to sewer under the following legislation:

Public Health Act 1936
Public Health (Drainage of Trade Premises) Act 1937
Public Health Act 1961
Water Act 1973
Control of Pollution Act 1974

Fig. 12.1 Extract from Hereford City Council's Register of Regulations

CHECKLIST

- *Is there a procedure for recording legislative requirements?*
- *Does the procedure document relevant environmental aspects of your company's activities?*
- *Is the register available where it is needed?*
- *Is the register regularly updated?*
- *Is the procedure comprehensive?*
  - *Assessed existing company records?*
  - *Focused on waste management practices?*
  - *Raw materials supply, its products and by-products?*
  - *Looked at key business processes and measurements?*
  - *Safety requirements.*
  - *Local authorities – requirements for control of accidents and emergencies.*
  - *Consents – NRA and LA consents for discharges.*
  - *Licences to deposit, treat or dispose of waste.*
  - *Duty of care – waste management procedures.*
  - *APC – air discharges and consents.*
  - *EPA (1990) – wastes, processes and discharges.*
  - *Major Accident Hazard Regulations – accidents and consequential limitations.*
  - *Water Resources Act 1991 – use, contamination and control.*
  - *Dangerous substances (1990) – notification and marking of sites.*
  - *Hazardous Substances (1990) – site plans and substances lists.*

Communication requirements of the environmental effects

The purpose of the environmental effects, communications requirement of BS7750 is to ensure that organisations take appropriate notice of the views and opinions of interested parties when formulating the environmental objectives and targets. The interested parties can be anyone with an interest in the environmental effect of your activities, products or services. This can mean *everyone* from the regulators to the staff, from the bank to the neighbours, from the customers to the insurance company, and *everything* from the raw materials sourcing to the disposal of the packaging, from the plant effluent to the distribution system, from the site services to the annual report.

Primarily then, the environmental effects requirement necessitates (a) a procedure to capture the communications received from people and organisations outside the company, (b) a system to document those communications and (c) a system to respond to those communications.

It is not necessary to respond to every inquiry or complaint of your company's environmental effects. You only need be concerned with 'relevant' interested parties and these will vary depending on the nature of your business. It may be relevant to manage communications with your local authority or the local Inspector of Pollutants, or to demonstrate to the local fire officer that your company has in place appropriate emergency action plans. It may be relevant to consider the requirements of your site neighbours, or to liaise with local environmental groups, or simply to understand the environmental concerns of your staff, customers or suppliers. What is crucial, however, is that you demonstrate in your communications procedures that you care and are committed.

THE COMMUNICATIONS PROCEDURE

Within the project you will have identified one person with responsibilities for communications, and this person should be the owner of the environmental communications process. The process should be designed to ensure that all communications are channelled to an appropriate owner for a response. The incoming communications will vary in source and in the interface with the organisation. For example, they may be telephone calls, correspondence, meetings or customer complaints and they may be directed towards senior management, middle management or to activities on the shop floor. From whatever source you need a centralised control point to track the incoming communications, apportion responsibility to the appropriate department and to action measures to ensure an adequate response.

The control point will need access to centres of competence throughout the organisation, which will answer the issues raised and report back to the control point what action has been taken. A documentation system should record each communication, track turnaround times and specify reporting measures throughout the process. The process must also identify who is responsible for receiving, documenting and responding to the issues raised. Again, it is job holders, not individuals, that must be recognised.

Senior management will also want to monitor the progress of communications to ensure that responses and appropriate records are kept. They should be kept informed of the issues raised and the actions taken.

Figure 12.2 demonstrates the communications procedure.

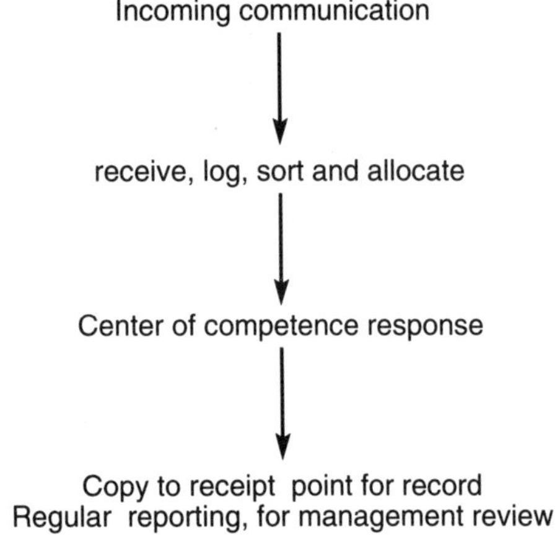

Fig. 12.2 Procedure for environmental effects communications

Examples

IBM have an internal communications programme called 'Speak up!' which allows issues to be raised by staff on a confidential basis. This is a form of safety valve, but it allows management to track the nature of issues concerning the staff.

Only the 'Speak up!' co-ordinator knows the origin of the letters. They are passed to the relevant executive for a response which is passed back through the same channel. If the employee is not satisfied, there can be a follow-up question. If anonymity is not an issue, they can arrange a face-to-face meeting at any level in the company.

As a barometer of employee feelings, the 'Speak up!' programme always included pay and compensation near the top, but in the 1980s and 1990s environmental issues rose in prominence. Policy matters relating to recycling, conserving energy, protecting wildlife, air pollution and use of CFCs were some of the topics concerning employees. Publication of more information at a general level in the company newsletter and the 'Programmes for the 90s' booklet, which consolidates all the environmental plans, has had the effect of reducing environmental 'Speak ups!' to a trickle.

The Body Shop uses a network of Environmental Advisers in shops to act as communication focus points to disseminate news and examples of good practice. A series of campaigns highlight The Body Shop's commitment to the environment that is an integral part of the corporate philosophy.

British Telecom focuses communications at particular target audiences to ensure that appropriate messages are available: shareholders through annual reports; employees through training programmes; customers and the local community through product labelling and project sponsorship; and suppliers through the publication of an environmental purchasing policy.

CHECKLIST

- *Do you have a documented procedure for managing communications?*
- *Does that procedure indicate who is responsible for:*
  - *receiving communications from interested parties?*
  - *documenting the communications received?*
  - *responding to the interested parties?*
- *Have you identified the centres of competence for areas of environmental inquiry?*
- *Do you have a plan for communications in crisis?*
- *Have you identified the areas of risk and assessed possible scenarios of environmental failure?*

- *Have you identified possible audiences for communications, and the mechanisms for communication?*

COMMUNICATION HINTS

In order to convince others that you are serious about environmental management issues remember the CAT factors:

- **Commitment** to the improvement of your environmental performance will be shown by the things you do, not the things you say. You must have evidence of the actions you are taking.
- **Accuracy** in the message is important, you must be consistent and truthful.
- **Trust** is the objective. The public want to trust you, but there is a fear of the unknown that is real and must be eased effectively. You must explain in language that the recipient can understand, not your jargon.

The environmental effects evaluation and register

The purpose of the environmental effects requirement of BS7750 is to ensure that the activities, products and processes of an organisation are assessed so that the EMS delivers appropriate standards of performance. Effects analysis is the core of the management system. The policy may set the scope and vision of the company's environmental goals; the management organisation may identify roles; the objectives, programme, manuals and controls will implement; audit and review assess performance, but the effects analysis takes you into new areas. It establishes where the effort should be spent to improve environmental performance and, for some, establishes for the first time what the performance is. You must establish criteria for identifying the environmental effects significant to your particular area of business or industry by undertaking various analysis procedures.

The results of the environment evaluation procedures must be recorded in a register which summarises the extent and scope of evaluation and 'signposts' where more detailed information will be found.

Environmental effects register

The register will bring together all the information on the environmental evaluation of the organisation's activities in a comprehensive reference document. This may be a part of the environmental management manual in a small organisation. In a larger organisation with a significant amount of data, it may be a separate document or documents, these should be referred to in the environmental management manual.

The register should include the following aspects with regard to the environmental effects evaluation documentation.

- Why the product or activity is deemed significant for evaluation of the environmental effects
- Who is responsible for the evaluation procedure
- What is the scope of the evaluation
- How the evaluation was carried out, and a summary of the results
- Where the procedure and records are available
- When the evaluation was carried out, and is due to be reviewed

ENVIRONMENTAL EFFECTS EVALUATION PROCEDURES

The preliminary review (see chapter 7) provided basic information on the activities of the organisation, established potential environmental effects and recommended areas of further analysis. Now you need to integrate environmental effects analysis into the day-to-day business procedures at two levels:

1. **General.** The 'searchlight' sweep that assesses, at a high level, the current status of environmental performance. This needs to be broad and look beyond the current environmental programmes and pressures to assess new issues, new directions in legislation, and potential pressures from stakeholders, the local community, market forces, etc. The management review process (see chapter 19) addresses this requirement.

2. **Specific.** Environmental effect evaluation procedures that vary according to the issues and activities under examination. For example:

   Products: life cycle assessment
   Projects: environmental impact assessments

Sites: site environmental audit
Processes: process assessment techniques (PAT)
Acquisition: due diligence audits
Risk: risk assessment procedures
Specific waste or emissions assessments

The expression 'environmental auditing' has now passed into common usage, and, as discussed in the introduction, the BS7750 is clear about the types of audit it sees as necessary to support the implementation of environmental management systems. All of the environmental effect assessment procedures described below can be called an environmental audit. The key factor that differentiates the type of audit from critical success, is the *scope* of the activity. Like all projects, and an environmental effects assessment or audit is another form of project, the terms of reference are essential. Set the scope, schedule and resources, action, reporting and follow-up for each assessment procedure at the outset.

Product assessment

The most commonly used form of environmental audit for product assessment is the life-cycle analysis or cradle-to-grave assessment. This is well established with several national product labelling schemes in Canada (Environmental Choice), Germany (Blue Angel), Japan (Eco-mark), Scandinavia (White Swan), and now the EC eco-label scheme of which the UK is a member. Companies can only display eco-labels if products reach certain pre-determined environmental standards.

Scope: The scope of an assessment must define clearly the product type and range, the key environmental criteria to be considered, and the product's fitness for purpose. For example, a washing machine may be very efficient in water, energy and detergent use, it is also required to wash clothes to certain standards.

The criteria should be relevant to global issues and include the methodology to be used to select criteria of significance.

Schedule and resources: The plan to assess the product should follow a pre-determined programme designed to test the product against the criteria defined in the scope. Adequate resources, from appropriately independent sources must be made available e.g. the use of BSI Testing.

Each step in the life cycle may require a different assessment approach, for example raw materials sourcing may require research, whereas the finished product performance can be physically tested.

Action: Assess product performance in all the life cycle areas:

- raw materials; where do materials come from, what are the potential effects, is there any choice?
- pre-production processes; what are the significant effects? Where does it start and stop? How much influence does your organisation have?
- production processes; distribution; what are the significant effects? What can be done to improve? Reduce energy use, pollution, waste, transport? Are we using the best available techniques, not exceeding excessive cost? Are we using the best environmental option? Can I reduce my cost impacts?
- utilisation; what are the effects in use? How does it compare with others?
- disposal; what are the effects? Can I re-use or re-cycle?

As an example, Fig. 12.3 shows the EC eco-label scheme matrix.

Reporting: Focuses on the performance of the product against the pre-set criteria. In the case of eco-labelling schemes, these criteria are usually set for particular issues that are shown to be significant for particular product groups.

Follow-up: Results from the product analysis are fed into the product development activities to ensure that the environmental performance criteria for the product are incorporated into the design process.

Example

Figure 12.4 shows The Body Shop's life cycle assessment approach used in the retail area.

Projects assessment

The prime UK legislative driver for product analysis techniques is the EC Directive (85/337/EEC) adopted in 1985, implemented in the Town and Country Planning Act (Assessment of Environmental Effects) Regulations 1988 – Statutory Instrument 1199/88.

Many organisations use this type of assessment procedure to analyse the environmental effects of site development planning applications or project reviews.

INDICATIVE ASSESSMENT MATRIX					
Product life cycle / Environmental fields	Pre-production	Production	Distribution (including packaging)	Utilisation	Disposal
Waste relevance					
Soil pollution and degradation					
Water contamination					
Air contamination					
Noise					
Consumption of energy					
Consumption of natural resources					
Effects on eco-systems					

Scoring system: 0 = nil pollution. 1: moderate 2: considerable

Fig 12.3 An EC eco-audit matrix

Scope: Is determined to establish the extent to which the environmental statement will address the existing environment and the effects of the proposed project.

Schedule and resources: Will involve detailed discussions with the relevant planning authority, where appropriate. If an internal company process, the plan will help define the issues to be examined and reported (as well as make it clear those areas that will not).

Action: includes descriptions of the project or proposed activity and the existing environmental situation before the project or proposed change is implemented, an analysis of the effect of the project or change on the

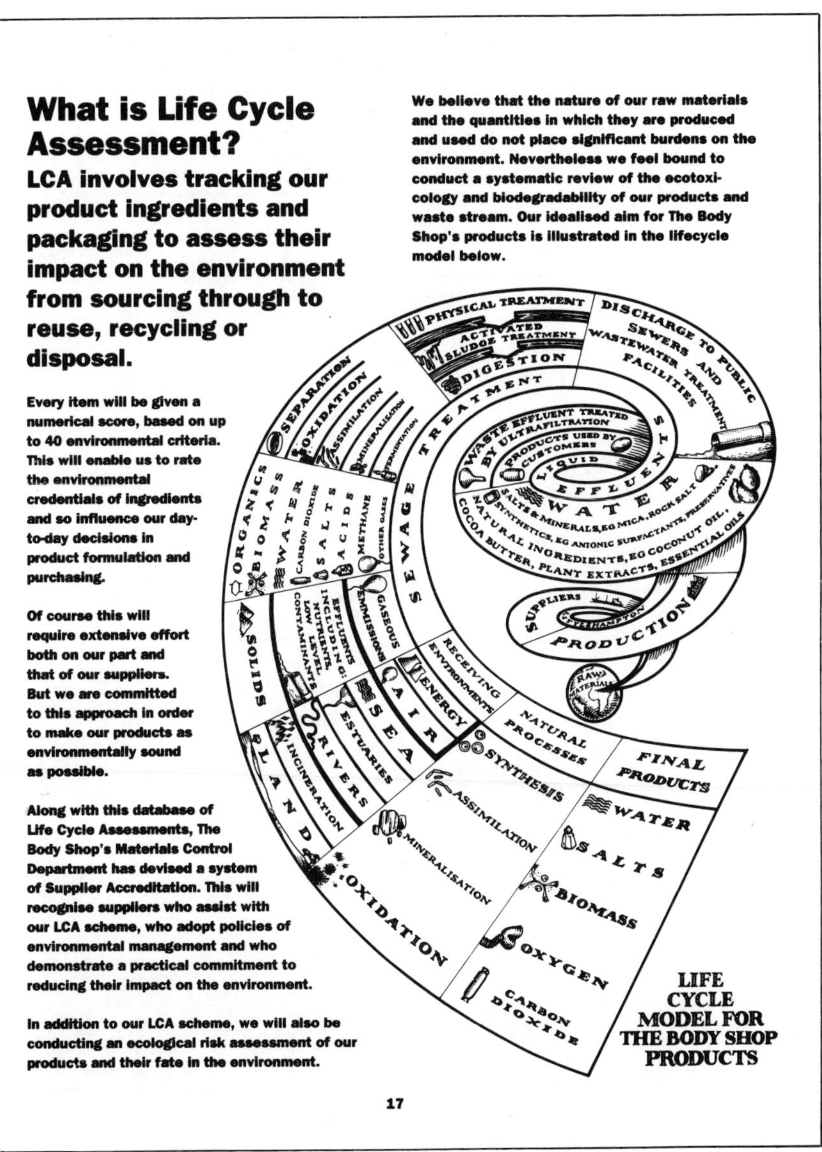

What is Life Cycle Assessment?

LCA involves tracking our product ingredients and packaging to assess their impact on the environment from sourcing through to reuse, recycling or disposal.

We believe that the nature of our raw materials and the quantities in which they are produced and used do not place significant burdens on the environment. Nevertheless we feel bound to conduct a systematic review of the ecotoxicology and biodegradability of our products and waste stream. Our idealised aim for The Body Shop's products is illustrated in the lifecycle model below.

Every item will be given a numerical score, based on up to 40 environmental criteria. This will enable us to rate the environmental credentials of ingredients and so influence our day-to-day decisions in product formulation and purchasing.

Of course this will require extensive effort both on our part and that of our suppliers. But we are committed to this approach in order to make our products as environmentally sound as possible.

Along with this database of Life Cycle Assessments, The Body Shop's Materials Control Department has devised a system of Supplier Accreditation. This will recognise suppliers who assist with our LCA scheme, who adopt policies of environmental management and who demonstrate a practical commitment to reducing their impact on the environment.

In addition to our LCA scheme, we will also be conducting an ecological risk assessment of our products and their fate in the environment.

17

Fig. 12.4 The Body Shop's life-cycle assessment in the retail area
Source: The Green Book, Body Shop International, 1992.

existing environment, and an analysis of the possible mitigating measures to reduce the anticipated environmental effect or to enhance any beneficial environment effects.

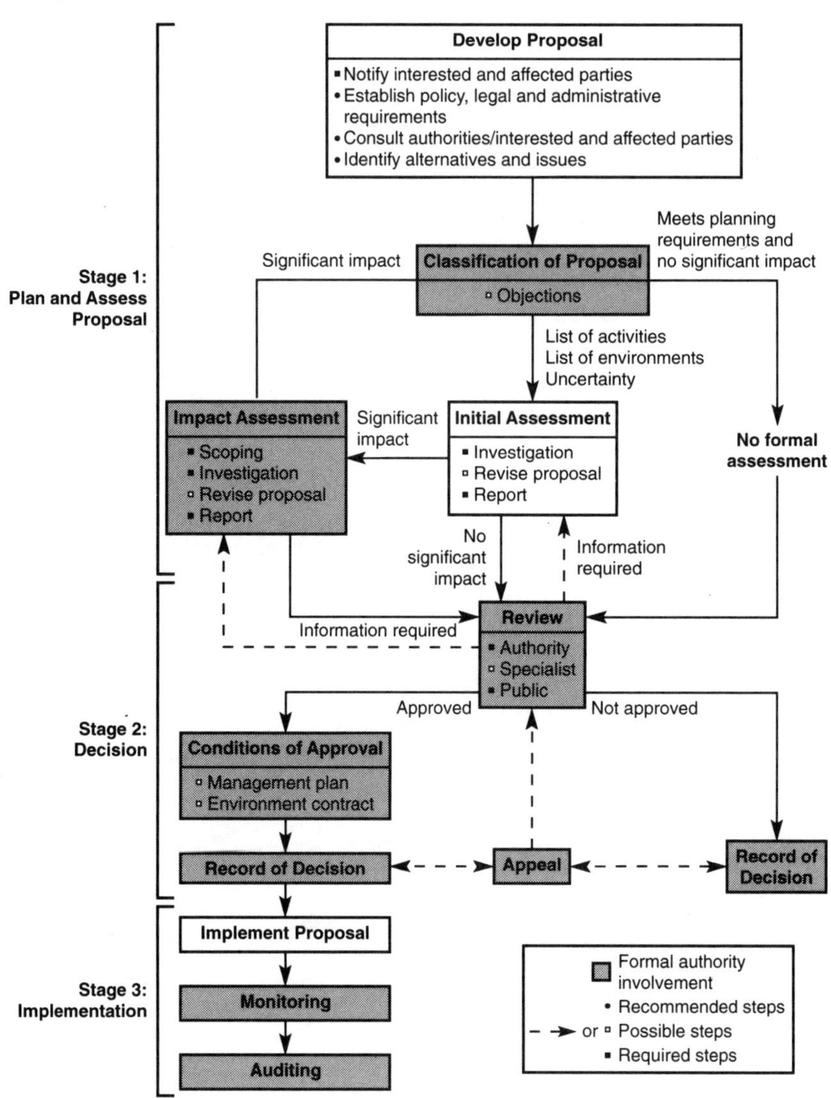

Fig. 12.5 An IEM procedure

Reporting: In legislative terms this is called the 'environmental statement'. It will include all the information indicated in the action phase, as well as a 'non-technical' summary explaining in simple terms the project intent, the environmental impact and recommended mitigating measures.

Follow-up: Includes the introduction of those mitigating factors, agreed at the report stage, into the project proposals and actions. Monitoring will be needed to ensure that the planned impact levels are accurate, and some form of corrective action may be needed to if the project impact is to be constrained within the predicted targets.

Site assessment

See chapter 7, preliminary review for guidance.

Process analysis

These can include formal process analysis using flow chart methods through to empirical methods devised to suit the business needs of individual organisations. Any business process from a production activity to an administrative activity can be analysed by understanding the various process steps as activities that have an input, added value and an output.

Scope: Defines the extent of the process being assessed. How far upstream and downstream you plan to go. Map out the process in diagrammatic form using a 'tree' diagram or similar.

EG 'Wash trucks' describes a process to clean owned and rented trucks. It has a number of activities from truck arrival, parking, drive-through wash, under-chassis steam clean, hand wash facility for trailers, parking, inspection and departure.

Responsibility for the operation comes under a single manager.

Schedule and resources: Plan the necessary effort and skill mix to look at all the aspects of the process. Establish the assessment criteria to look at the process against a matrix that relates the activities to global issues. This will allow you to assess the specific environmental loads and possible directions for improvement.

The pro-forma matrix requires consideration of the primary effects of an activity. Does it use energy? Has it got problems of greenhouse gas production or resource use of fossil fuels? Does it use lots of water or chemicals which can deplete resources or risk pollution incidents.

Action: Using the assessment criteria, measure the actual performance. It will involve looking at the steps in the process and seeing the actual effects on the various media (air, water and land), looking at the use of resources, wastes and energy, and the effects on special habitats. Record the findings and assess possible actions to improve performance. Use the ratings as a tool to decide which are the more significant.

Example

PROCESS ACTIVITY	ENVIRONMENTAL EFFECT	GLOBAL ISSUE	MEASURE	POLICY PRIORITY
INPUT				
Parking	diesel spills	pollution	freq/vol	reduce 1
ACTIVITIES				
Wash	energy	$CO_2/NO_x/SO_x$ resources	volume costs	reduce 2
Steam clean	water	resources	volume	reduce 3 reuse
	effluent	pollution	volume	control 2
	chemical	pollution	volume type	reduce 3 reuse
OUTPUTS				
Parking	diesel spills	pollution	freq/vol	reduce 1

Reporting: The report to management will provide the data to be built into the EMS skeleton on effects, measurements and activities to form the action plan.

The summary of the truck wash assessment might result in a report that recommended action in the area of chemicals management, water recycling and reuse. Energy use from the steam cleaner and improved control of spills in the wash area and 'carry-off' by trucks out of the area.

Follow-up: Might include actions to set targets and management responsibilities for water and energy savings, or to establish better control over chemicals use and wastes. The objectives are integrated into those of the line managers and staff as well as into any cross-functional service agreements, like the site services personnel. Key points are held over for the next system audit and review.

CHECKLIST

Register of environmental effects

- *Is there a procedure for determining your environmental effects requirements?*
- *Have you documented your findings in an environmental effects register?*
- *Does the register describe the status quo?*
- *Does the register describe the activity being assessed in a clearly defined scope clause?*
  project – extent and boundaries of the project activity.
  process – extent for the process input to output.
  product – extent of the product life, upstream and downstream.
- *Is the register regularly reviewed?*

COMMUNICATION HINTS

- In assessing those areas of activity for inclusion in the effects register and scoring high in significance criteria, it is worth considering the 80/20 formulae. This will indicate that 80% of the environmental burdens will probably come from 20% of your activities. While all aspects of the organisation must be assessed, the 80/20 approach will ensure you are addressing the significant activities.
- The register should be accessible to all employees to demonstrate the commitment to the environmental policy for continual improvement. It will, over time, show the improvement in performance.
- When reviewing the results of environmental evaluations, include a commentary on the process itself, as well as the results. It will allow you to improve the assessment procedures when it is time for a re-evaluation.

13

Environmental objectives and targets

The purpose of this requirement of BS7750 is to ensure that there are clear environmental goals within the organisation as a whole and for each departmental management team. The guidance to BS7750 indicates that the goals should be set to achieve a year-on-year improvement but not necessarily in every area of activity, i.e. they are strategic and not short-term. The environmental effects analysis of the organisation will indicate areas for improvement so there is a clear and discernible link from policy, effects evaluation and improvement targets.

The targets should be demanding, in that they should require special efforts to achieve them. There is little point in setting targets at low levels as they provide little motivation or satisfaction on achievement. However, it is always useful to have some early wins to report when you know that it will be important to show how well some people are doing. Objectives and targets should be quantified wherever this is practical to ensure that real attainment is recorded against the targets.

OBJECTIVE

The goal is a comprehensive set of objectives and targets, from the boardroom to the shop floor, integrated into the day-to-day business activities of the managers and staff. The objectives and targets must be motivational so that staff can see management practising policy application.

Establishing environmental objectives and targets

If we look at the characteristics of activity management in organisations we find that the business processes (invoicing, tank cleaning, environmental measurements) are not 'owned' by the operator, but by the accounts departments, managers or technical experts. Very often the results of environmental monitoring go to the expert rather than the operator. The operator may get a report only when an emission exceeds a set alarm level. He or she may not receive a trend chart which shows when things are deviating from normal standards.

The idea behind setting environmental objectives and targets is to enable all staff, at every relevant level of the company, to have personal goals for improving environmental standards. Staff should be involved in a total quality approach to environmental management. The use of the interactive implementation workshop to set targets is an effective way to achieve this at all levels of an organisation, from the senior executive team down through the various departments to the shop floor. Managers and staff work together in a non-threatening way to look at *how* things are done – a good technique for highlighting gaps or overlaps in management systems. The result, a management system review with an environmental focus, which will lead to action plans to improve environmental performance in day-to-day operations.

In setting targets and objectives, the workshops should take the following into account:

- compliance with all legislative and regulatory requirements as specified in the departmental register of the same;
- other objectives and targets documented in the environmental register;
- the financial, operational and business requirements;
- the views of interested parties; and
- the general environmental policy statement of the company.

The environmental targets must be documented, realistic time-scales for completion should be set and managers and staff alike should monitor progress to achieving the targets within the time-frame. Remember that objectives and targets should be consistent with environmental policy and quantify wherever possible to the commitment to continual improvement in environmental performance.

Example

Figure 13.1 is an extract from Wessex Water's action plan which sets out the company's objectives for improving its environmental performance.

4 The action plan

4.1 *Putting principles into practice*

We will put our principles into practice by:

- *setting environmental improvement objectives for every part of the company, involving appropriate members of staff*
- *working at achieving sustainable environmental performance*
- *publishing the results of our environmental performance*
- *explaining to customers the importance of the environment and the steps – some requiring their help – being taken to secure improvement*
- *continuing to support schools and colleges in the education of young people on environmental conservation*
- *liaising and co-operating with other bodies involved in environmental protection*
- *seeking long term, sustainable development, not short term gain.*

Fig. 13.1 Extract from Wessex Water's action plan

Qualifying environmental objectives and targets

From the implementation workshop and the environmental effects analysis the areas for objectives and targets will be focused. To manage improvement in these areas some form of quantifiable measurement is essential – 'if you can't measure it you can't manage it'. Terms like minimise effluents and maximise recycling are vague.

These measurements may be specific at a strategic level aimed at general policy; for example: reduce air emissions by 10 per cent over 1990 levels by the end of 1993. For a specific function, this may be translated into: implement a project to install catalytic converters to clean air emissions from production line A, or an objective to change adhesive material from solvent based to water based in a defined timescale.

The quantification is usually easy in technical areas; chemical oxygen demand (COD) of effluent can be measured and tracked; amounts of effluent sludge can be recorded as well as the percentage of chemical content in waste waters. Electrical consumption and cost of waste can be calculated in providing real benefits in achieving reduction.

Physical actions can also be measured; bunding of effluent filtration

table 1: examples of policy areas and objectives

policy area	corporate objectives
Good neighbour	Reduce impacts in all key performance areas
Effluent/emissions * Minimise air emissions/effluent Reduce air emissions/effluent Improve emissions control/effluent treatment	 Achieve optimum effluent in relation to production Reduce by 10% by end of 1992 Implement improvements by end of 1992
Waste * Minimise waste Reduce waste Increase level of recycling	 Reduce average daily weight of waste to landfill by 20 tonnes Reduce waste by 5% by end of 1992 Recycle 100% of recyclable materials
Energy Reduce consumption Improve energy efficiency	 Reduce energy consumption per unit of production Reduce energy consumption by 15% by 1995 against 1990 as base year Implement energy efficiency measures
Natural Resources Minimise damage to natural habitats Reduce the use of material resources	 Ensure all new materials from sustainable sources Reduce water use by 25%
Suppliers Actively influence performance of suppliers	 Purchase from least polluting suppliers Raise awareness of all suppliers by 1993
Products Develop, manufacture and market products that are safe, energy efficient, and which can be recycled or disposed of safely	 Eliminate all hazardous materials by 1995 Improve recyclability to 90% by vehicle weight Reduce average disassembly time to 20 minutes
Internal Investment Invest in best available technology to address pollution problems	 Invest 10% of turnover in environmental improvements for the next 3 years.
External Investments Ensure only investment in environmentally sound companies and projects.	 Transfer 100% of investment portfolio to environmentally responsible projects and companies by the end of 1994
Corporate relations Public openness Support for environmental programmes	 Implement mechanism for public disclosure and consultation by end of 1992 Achieve active participation in industry environment Implement on-going programme for sponsorship and donations.

**In this document we employ the following conventions:*

- *emissions refer to air pollution;*
- *effluent relates to discharges to watercourses or sewers;*
- *waste refers to 'controlled' or 'non-controlled' waste disposed of to landfill or incineration.*

Fig. 13.2

Source: 'A Measure of Commitment – guidelines on Measuring Environmental Performance', Business in the Environment and KPMQ, Peat Marwick, available from BiE.

systems, oil tanks or hydrogen peroxide tanks are done/not done; projects to install vapour recovery systems installed and the amount of recycled material in products can be tracked.

Administration improvements are more difficult. These can include establishing management systems; emergency recovery systems; suppliers' and contractors' compliance with your policy and codes of practice. These can include the contribution of turnover to environmental investment, the beginnings of environmental accounting.

Examples of policy areas and objectives are shown in the extract from *A Measure of Commitment*, 1992 – Business in the Environment.

CHECKLIST

- *Do the objectives and targets establish realistic and meaningful improvements?*
- *Have you used all available documentation in establishing your objectives and targets?*

- *Can they be properly quantified?*
- *Are there areas where more information is needed to establish objectives and targets?*

COMMUNICATION HINTS

- Within the organisation, the resulting objectives and targets can be communicated as part of the regular process to update progress towards the strategic policy implementation.
- External communications can be done through a booklet or brochure which will explain the link between the policy, objectives, targets and the resulting actions that will effect suppliers, contractors, customers and other external interested parties.
- Regular reporting is important to ensure that progress is maintained against the benchmark, tracking the views of interested parties to ensure that the appropriate issues are being addressed.

14

The environmental programme

The purpose of this requirement of BS7750 is to ensure that within the organisation the policy goals, objectives and targets are supported by a realistic programme for implementation. The programme will exist at every level where objectives and targets have been set. In large organisations, therefore, there will be several 'layers' of programmes and these should be related. For example, an organisation may, at a national level, set a target of reducing the waste that goes to landfill by 20 per cent over a twelve-month period. But at a site level one might expect to find different programmes for the same objective. These would relate to the type and amount of waste generated, the maturity of site management in improving waste streams and the capacity of local suppliers/removers to respond to a switch to more recycling.

OBJECTIVE

The establishment of a co-ordinated implementation programme throughout the organisation to achieve the company's environmental objectives and targets.

Implementation programmes

Each workshop group that developed objectives and targets must have an implementation programme to go with it. The plan should include milestones to be achieved against key dates and the activities necessary to make it happen. Programmes will vary according to the products, processes and activities involved. For example, environmental objectives to improve a continuous process like a paper mill have a different type of programme from environmental objectives to improve a construction project. In the paper process, the objective might be to achieve a higher standard of waste water purity, which may be dependent on a particular change in the process involving the installation of new equipment. The programme will show a 'step' improvement planned to occur when particular plant or equipment is installed. In the construction industry the objective might be how to achieve waste reduction targets, transport savings or noise containment targets that are heavily dependent on changes in the behaviour of operatives. This programme will show a planned 'graded' improvement, linked to education, training and the application of new operating procedures.

The role of the environmental programme manager is to ensure that the key milestones of each 'sub-programme' are linked to a realistic overview that demonstrates a movement towards meeting the targets. It is important that the programme identifies responsibilities, methods, and measures. The programme will not just list the things to be done; it will also state who is responsible, when plans will be achieved and how the owner (and everyone else) will know they have been achieved.

A lot of your time could be spent chasing information to ensure that you know that the overview programme is correct, and that the sub-programmes are maintaining momentum. In addition to owning the achievement of the sub-programmes, you should ensure that the departmental co-ordinators own the maintenance of their parts of the overview programme. For example, in your regular management progress review meetings you will ask each functional or departmental head to make a report of his or her own progress, while you report on the overall achievements.

A structural approach to implementation programmes

The implementation workshop and the departmental EMS skeleton have identified the key activities, ownership, dates and criteria that form the environmental programme. The method to integrate these into a common programme is the use of a structured approach which ensures some consistency in the presentation of the material. If all implementation programmes follow the same sequence of steps, you will find it easier to monitor progress and fit all the activities into your general overview. All projects go through phases, and these can be set-up as 'gates' against which reports are made. For example:

Step 1: Identification

Understand the problem at greater depth through analysing the data. Understand the complexity, resource requirement, availability, impacts and potential timing. The 'output' at this stage is a formal 'problem statement' – a simple and succinct statement which captures the essence of what will be changed as a result of the activity. It is equivalent to a scope statement for a project.

Step 2: Analysis

Determine the root cause of the problem. This may involve gathering further data, specific analysis techniques and some testing to ensure that the causes of the problem are properly understood. The 'output' at this stage is an expanded problem statement that is specifically focused on the root causes.

Step 3: Solution development

Determine the changes necessary to resolve the root cause of the problem. Define the solution *criteria* if the problem is to be successfully eliminated. Review solution options and select 'best fit' to the criteria. Carry out tests or pilot activities to prove the proposed solution. The 'output' at this stage is a proposal which meets the solution criteria. Obtain the necessary approvals and establish a project plan for implementation, which should now be communicated.

Step 4: Implementation

Plan and manage the solution project plan so that you remove the inhibitors to the improvement you seek. The 'output' at this stage will be changes in the practices, processes and procedures necessary to achieve the improvement.

Step 5: Review

Check that the solution which has been put in place has solved the problem. This means going back to the original measurements to check that the new procedure has resulted in the right kind of changes. The 'output' at this stage will be a report demonstrating the achievement against the original criteria.

Establishing a protocol for the phased implementation to improve environmental standards as a mechanism for measuring progress against the plans. If you want the protocol programme to be effective, it must combine a sensible, structured approach that implementors will use because it helps them, and the correct elements to ensure that you can track what is happening. The implementors can then regard the five stages as 'gates' that must be passed through, if the environmental objectives and targets are to be implemented. Each sub-project is, at any one time, somewhere along the path.

Remember the 'off-target' approach to problem-solving. Do not make each step such an onerous activity that progress and enthusiasm are inhibited. It is better to run through quickly and then improve the performance from a new level than to 'nit-pick' the progress through the stages.

Example

RH Technical Industries, use a PC based structured format shown in illustration 14.1. Project managers responsible for implementing a project can use the form to indicate:

The project overview,
The team and team leader,
The planned project steps and dates and
The actual achievement.

The legend provides not only a convenient way to show the project steps, but provides some discipline to the phases to be undertaken.

The priorities within implementation programmes

PRIORITIES OF THE 7-S MODEL

One of the points that emerges from the 7-S approach to implementing change programmes is that tensions can arise if the changes are not implemented across the whole company. By prioritising the activities of

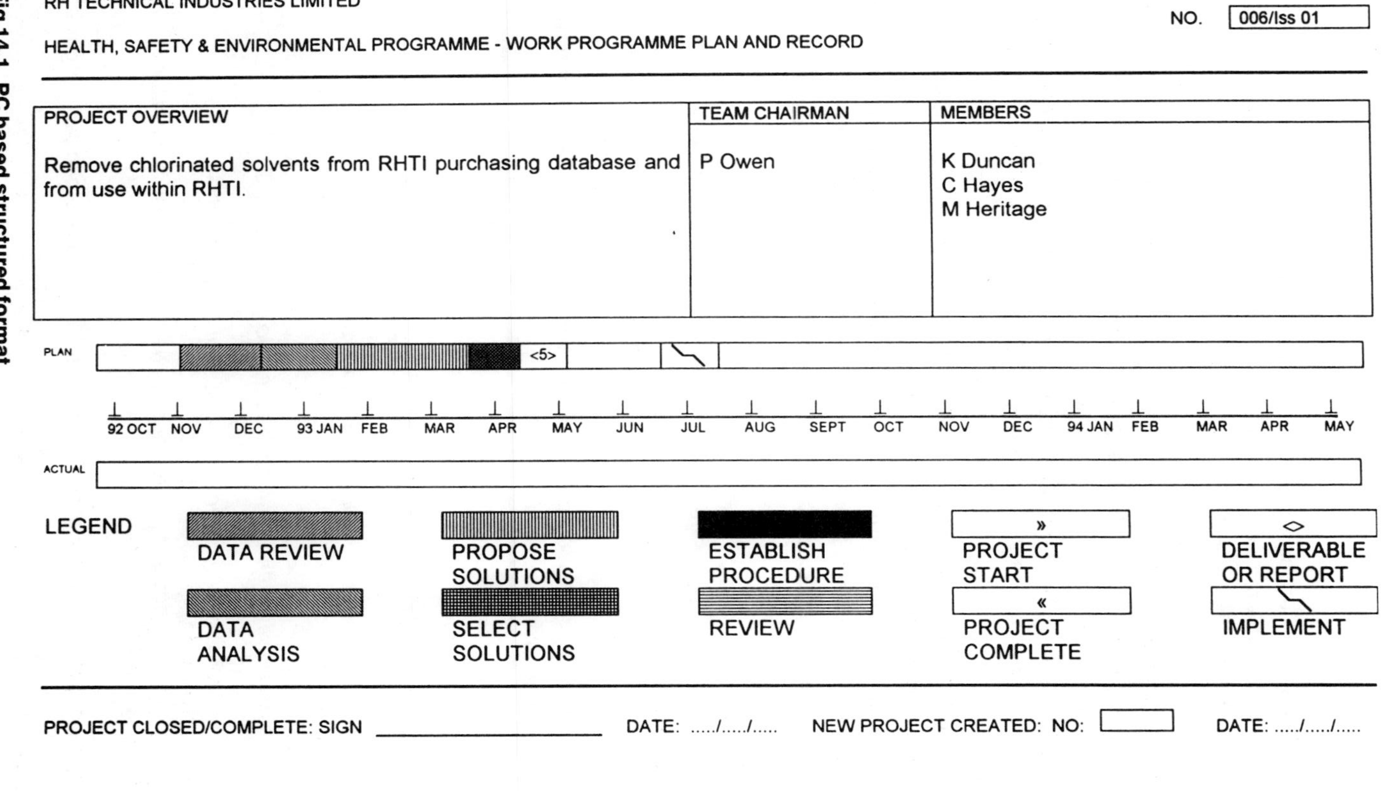

Fig 14.1 PC based structured format

Source: RH Technical Industries Ltd. Developed by Chris Hills OPS, DIR for RH Technical Industries Ltd, Winchester.

the implementation programme you can reduce the likelihood of the transitional problems that may arise. Based on the guidelines of the 7-S model, these priorities are:

1. **Strategy:** the strategic elements of your environmental policy is the starting point. Does the programme reflect the broad aims of the company?
2. **Skills:** You must have the skills necessary to make the changes happen. Are the skills you need in place or, if not, have you made provision to acquire them?
3. **Staff:** You must balance the staff resources you have against the simplicity or complexity of the systems you propose to introduce. Are the staff equipped to meet the new processes and practices?
4. **Systems:** You must have systems in place to monitor and document the programme. Are new systems required and who is responsible for documenting and monitoring them?

5. **Structure:** You must establish roles, responsibilities and resources to implement the changes. Does the current management structure reflect the management and resources of the programme?
6. **Style:** You must adopt a motivational management style – reward success, encourage better performance and promote shared values. Does the organisation's culture allow and encourage the implementation of the programme?

CHECKLIST

- *Does the programme show how the objectives and targets will be met?*
- *Can you see the relationship and the links between the programme and the goals?*
- *Does each activity of the programme state who is responsible?*
- *Does the programme show how the targets will be achieved?*
- *Have you established a structured approach to ensure consistency of the implementation programmes across the company?*
- *Are the priorities clearly identified and relevant to the whole organisation's goals?*

COMMUNICATION HINTS

- Publishing the implementation programmes in the company newsletter and through your regular reports is a important way to ensure that staff commitment remains high.

- Make sure you have a visible programme with memorable dates from which it is difficult to default, even when the going gets tough!
- At regular reviews ensure the owners of the programme elements make the presentations on progress. After all, it is the co-ordinator's programme and he or she will want the plaudits when it is completed.
- Be open about changes or delays in progress; your reputation is built on trust in this area, inaccurate reporting damages your credibility.

15

Environmental management manual and documentation control

The purpose of this requirement of BS7750 is to ensure that there is adequate documentation to support the environmental management system in operation. In addition to the specified environmental management manual, all documentation relating to the EMS must be controlled. Controlled documentation is that which is necessary to ensure the effective operation of the practices and procedures by the organisation's management and staff. Documentation provides the foundation on which the EMS audit assesses compliance, and therefore has to be designed to meet all the requirements of the EMS and the Standards. If you imagine that wherever the Standard has a specification that calls for certain procedures to be present, an assessor, either internal or external, will ask to see the documentation that describes that procedure. Only when it is clear what the documented procedure is, will the next question follow . . . 'Please show me that what you say you do, is what you actually do'.

OBJECTIVE

The goal is to compile a set of documents that:

- **meets the requirements of the Standard;**
- **is effective in implementing environmental performance improvement;**
- **is integrated into the existing management system;**
- **includes a co-ordinating document, the environmental management manual.**

The importance of documentation

'Bureaucracy' is one of the most overused words in the business world. We complain about it, yet we know documents are essential. We would not buy a video machine or a car without documentation. We use contracts, invoices, letters, files and records every day to keep the business running. We create new ways of doing things every day, ask people to provide new measurements or different reports. Yet when we are asked to document *how* we get things done, up goes the cry 'bureaucracy'!

So, we must accept that documents need to exist. They are essential to the operation of the business. What is important, however, is to know what documentation is necessary: those that are essential must exist; only what you need should exist. The necessary documentation must be managed so that it is kept up to date and owned so that a specific job holder has responsibility to keep it up to date, change it, withdraw it, etc. This is known as 'documentation control'.

In addition, each document should be unique, i.e. it should have a specific purpose, be designed to meet that purpose, and should not duplicate another document or any part of another document. In the case of the environmental management manual this is particularly important. The manual will almost certainly refer to other documents in the organisation – reporting structures, operating instructions, protocols and procedures. If they are all repeated in the environmental management manual, it will be prohibitively expansive, expensive and impossible to keep up to date. The manual should be a very slim document.

Documentation must also be accessible and 'user friendly'. Barry Dale of ERL talks about 'dog-eared manuals' being the real test of a usable and appropriate documentation system. Each document should be written in plain English with short words, short sentences and the minimum of jargon. It must also be designed and written to suit its audience.

Example

The IBM property management function was installing a quality management system and decided to carry out a document inventory to understand what documentation the 300 employees considered as essential to the operation. It was found that over 40 documents were used regularly by staff, but of these, some were out of date, some were not used where they should have been and some had no ownership. Very few met BS5750's requirement of 'controlled documentation'. On completion of the project, however, the document inventory had reduced to 20 essential documents, each of which was current, had a defined owner and was available 'on line' or through an appropriate contact point. Thus, rather than increasing the company's bureaucracy, the implementation of the quality management system resulted in a reduced bureaucracy.

Many companies use on-line documentation, accessed through a networked computer system. This provides one of the key requirements for controlled documentation. If staff have access to a computer terminal they have access to all the documentation that they need and documents can be updated regularly and easily in such controlled circumstances.

The environment management manual

For an assessor, the assessment process will begin with a request to see the environmental management manual. He/she then evaluates whether the system you have in place is sufficiently comprehensive and mature to warrant a site visit. Assessors require documents to show what should be done, and records to demonstrate that it is being done. For example, if you have a particular process to monitor and record the handling and disposal of hazardous waste to meet the requirements of the Duty of Care legislation, the necessary documentation will be reviewed, and the activities and records assessed for compliance. In addition, the appropriateness of the environmental control practices and procedures will be considered, to ensure that, for example, the right test method is being used in the right place and is providing the appropriate management control.

The environmental management manual needs to be an established and maintained document that collates the environmental policy, the objectives and targets and the implementation programme. It must specify who is responsible for what areas of activity, how the system is designed to work, and must contain 'signposts' to other related documentation.

The manual (or manuals if its a large organisation) will cover the day-to-day activities, abnormal operating conditions, and incident, accident and emergency situations. It must ensure that emergency plans contain information and instructions that address environmental risks and pollution problems.

Compiling the environmental management manual

The implementation workshop, chapter 9, will generate the key information you need to document the EMS at every key level. Each department, function or branch will have a local EMS for the operational elements particularly relevant to them. At a higher level there will be a co-ordinating document that brings all the constituent parts together. Figure 15.1 shows the distribution of documentation within an organisational framework.

At each department level there is the local document designed around the common framework or 'skeleton'. Each should be a crisp concise document, directing you towards other common documentation, except where there are specific points relevant to the areas of responsibility of the department. At the higher level the documentation comprises common practices and procedures, standards, emergency plans, and management information systems which provide the necessary co-ordination of the operational elements. One of these will be the environmental management manual.

Each department is documenting the relationship of organisations environmental policy to its mission, plans, dependencies, deliverables, procedures, measurements and improvement programmes.

Of course, the environmental management manual must include documentation on all the relevant practices, procedures and activities to fulfil the BS7750 requirements and be a fully integrated element of the management system. It, and the other necessary documentation, must record effective activities in implementing, monitoring, reviewing and improving your company's environmental performance.

CHECKLIST: ENVIRONMENTAL MANAGEMENT MANUAL

- *Does the manual exist?*

  Does it contain: environmental policy; environmental objectives and targets; environmental programme; roles and responsibilities; and a description of the system.

- *Does the information cover abnormal operations?*

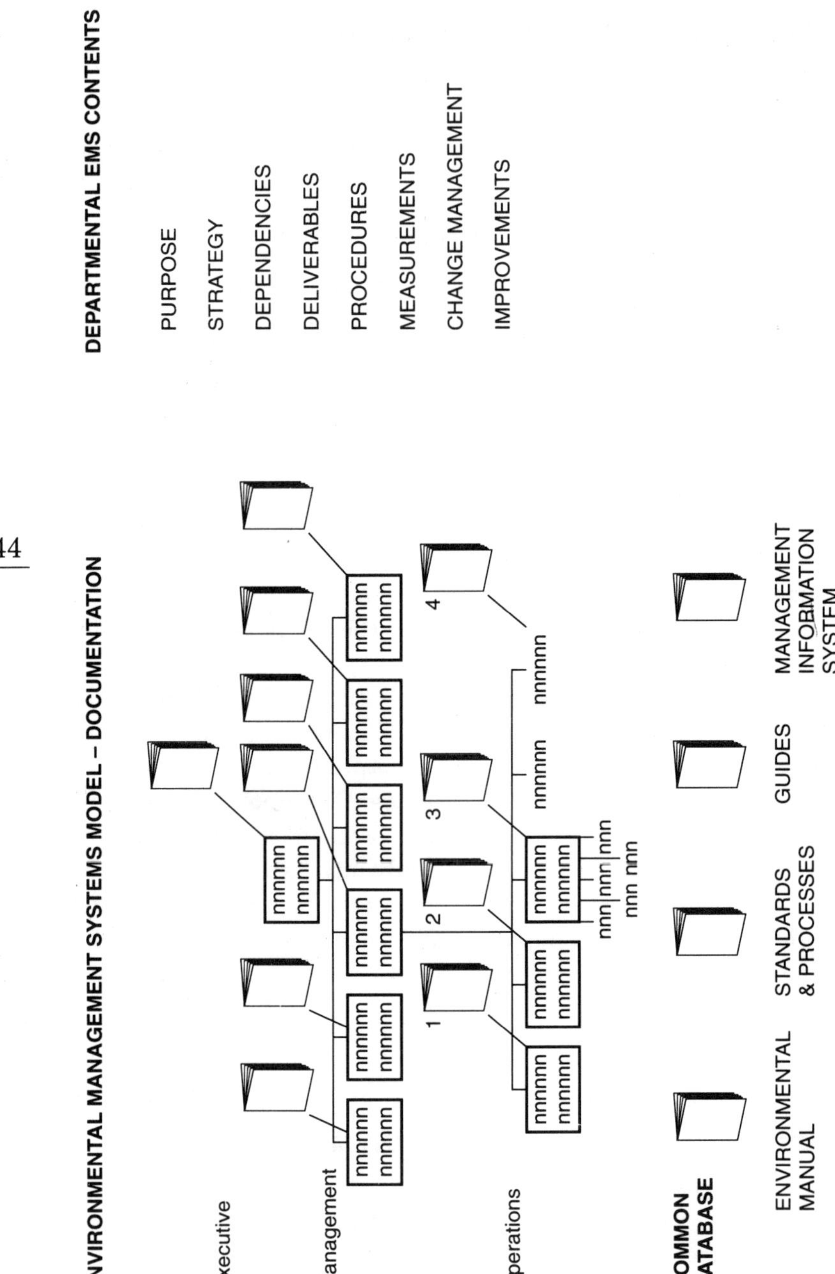

Fig. 15.1 The distribution of documentation within a structured framework

- *Does the information cover incidents, accidents and potential emergency operations?*
- *Do the emergency plans contain relevant environmental information.*

Procedures for controlling documentation

Part of the common database will be the document control procedures. This should be a brief summary of the appropriate procedures to ensure that documents are controlled. Your staff support functions may own a document like this, smaller organisations often find that sharing out the ownership of common processes between line managers provides a balance between tactical and strategic views. This has the added benefit of encouraging mutual support and co-operation. It also avoids the creation of large staff departments as an unproductive, but expensive burden, and usually ensures that the documentation you have is only the essential information – busy line managers do not create paperwork for the sake of it.

When preparing the documentation control document, the following factors should be considered:

1. Every document must have a purpose, whether to advise, guide, describe a process or report a requirement. The beginning of the document should define the scope, what it covers and what it does not.
2. Every document must have an owner. The owner is not an individual but a job-holder. For example the owner of the internal EMS audit may be the environmental programmes manager, not 'Bill Bloggs'.
3. Every document must have some method of indicating its currency – When it was last updated and when it will next be updated.
4. Every document must be available to those who need to refer to it in their day-to-day activities in support of the environmental objectives and targets.

Example

Figure 15.2 is an extract from Gleaner's EMS documentation. As a relatively small company it uses hardcopy documentation which is

ENVIRONMENTAL MANAGEMENT MANUAL

Gleaner OIL AND GAS

Page: 16
of: 26

GLEANER OILS LTD•MILNFIELD•ELGIN•MORAYSHIRE IV30 IUZ•TEL 0343-547977•TLX 4573205

REVISION	AMENDMENT	PREPARED BY	DATE	APPROVED BY	DATE
00	00	A. Buchanan	09/11/92		16/11/92

4.7 ENVIRONMENTAL MANAGEMENT MANUAL AND DOCUMENTATION

4.7.1 Manual

This manual defines the general environmental policy and refers to the Environmental Management Programme which also contains the company's environmental objectives and targets.

Additional detailed procedures which have been produced to set the standards for specific activities are listed in section 6.

Records generated by the environmental management system are identified in Section 7 of this manual and in other operational procedures.

4.7.2 Documentation

Environmental management system documentation is controlled in a similar manner to quality system documents and uses records of a similar format where possible.

The EM Coordinator shall ensure that all documented environmental management procedures have been approved by management prior to issue.

A Document Master List (Q01) of identifiying the current status of documented procedures shall be maintained by the EM Coordinator.

The EM Coordinator shall form a Distribution List (Q02) for each document recorded on the Master List.

All changes to the documents shall be reviewed and approved by management.

The EM Coordinator shall issue a Transmittal Note (Q03) to each holder when distributing a new document or an amendment to an existing document. The holder of the document shall acknowledge receipt of the document (and destruction of any superseded documents/pages) by signing and returning the Transmittal Note to the EM Coordinator.

The amendments shall be made by replacing relevant pages or by reissuing a complete copy of the document. Each amended page shall be identified by a manual revision level and a page amendment number and date.

Amendments are numbered consecutively until a revision of the manual incorporates all the changes. When the revised manual is issued the revision level will be raised by one increment and all amendment levels will be returned to zero.

An Amendment Log Sheet shall be included in the document to indicate all amendments which have been incorporated. Unauthorised amendments shall be prohibited.

Fig. 15.2 An extract from Gleaner's EMS documentation

available to a highly skilled staff who know their product is potentially an environmental hazard. It is available as a hardcopy, loose-leaf document around the organisation.

CHECKLIST: DOCUMENTATION

- *Is there an established and maintained documentation control procedure?*
- *Does the procedure cover*
  - *identification of documentation by division or function?*
  - *the scope of each document?*
  - *the current edition and next revision information?*
  - *change approval procedures?*
  - *name of the owner.*
- *Does the procedure indicate how access will be controlled?*
- *Does the procedure cover the withdrawal of obsolete documents?*

COMMUNICATION HINTS

- One of the problems that busy staff face is the 'help' they get from staff documents. Document owners must ensure that the users of documents have the opportunity to comment on what they will have to work with. Owners should listen to what the users say and reflect their views.
- Ensure 'readability' is implicit in the documents. Aim at a comprehension index appropriate to the recipients.
- Measure the use of documents regularly and set yardsticks for maintaining documents in circulation.
- Withdraw documents that do not meet your criteria for usage.
- Update and change documents immediately they are out of date. Your users will appreciate your commitment to accuracy.
- Aim at 'well thumbed' documentation.

16

Operational control

The purpose of this section of BS7750 is to ensure that the environmental policy, objectives, targets and programme are translated into action on a day-to-day basis throughout the organisation. The Standard has three main sub-clauses that cover:

- control procedures to ensure activities take place within appropriate parameters;
- verification, measurement and testing to ensure that the control procedures are effective;
- non-compliance and corrective action to change the control procedures when they fail.

All three are an integrated part of an effective operational control programme, but it is easier to understand the elements if we look at them separately.

Control

The expression 'controlled conditions' is used to define a designed state whereby production processes take place in predictable patterns, under the control of the operating staff. The expression is used for all operational procedures, whether manufacturing or administrative. The controlled state provides confidence to management and staff that, provided the operating instructions are followed, the process will operate within the design parameters. The product or service that forms the outcome of the process, will then meet the requirements of the organisation. The confidence in system performance then allows management to concentrate on improving the processes and products to higher standards, rather than just getting by.

The requirement of BS7750 does not ask for instructions for everything, everywhere, but it does ask for documented work instructions where the lack of them could result in a failure to achieve the environmental policy, objectives and targets. For example, if it is a part of your policy to ensure that your suppliers meet your environmental performance standards, you may need to tell your staff responsible for procurement that this is required. Your procurement process will reflect this (e.g. Boots and B&Q) and terms and conditions of your contracts will include references to your criteria. This is not just a case of adding BS7750 alongside the place in the contract where BS5750 is documented. You need to clarify the implications of the environmental standards you are looking for and the impact on the product and services you wish to receive.

Whereas BS5750 compliance assures that there is a quality system ensure you should get the products or services you specify, BS7750 may result in more wide-ranging changes in the supplier organisation which may have an impact on the specification you provide. In the pilot programme the Rover Group worked with a number of small suppliers to understand the implications of Rover asking for BS7750 compliance as a contract term. The results showed it is achievable, but it is not done just by adding BS7750 to the contract and forgetting the implications, both parties must work together.

If your policy includes a commitment to comply with the requirements of the EC Eco-Management and audit Regulation, then you will need to publish a regular environmental statement. Your staff will need to know who is responsible for what, when and how. If your targets include specific reductions in waste streams, you will need to instruct staff in how this will be measured and what is required of them. If your targets include reducing energy demands to reduce the CO_2 burden, then your instructions on the procurement of plant and equipment, building design standards, transport and product design will need to make that clear.

Although all parts of the organisation effect the environment, this requirement focuses on those activities that are relevant to the implementation of the environmental policy, objectives and targets. The documented work instructions should include guidance on operational activities, procurement and contracted activities, process control, planning and approval of new processes or equipment and the setting of environmental performance criteria.

OBJECTIVE

The goal is a set of documented practices, procedures and systems to ensure that the activities of the organisation, which have an impact on the environmental policy and targets, are carried out under controlled conditions.

Identification of the critical activities

The key to operational control procedures is the output from the implementation workshop and the functional/departmental EMS. These provide the identification of the critical activities, i.e. those which, if they went wrong, would most compromise your ability to deliver the environmental performance standards specified. To establish these critical activities, you must look at the environmental critical success factors (CSF) for the department/function. Follow the exercise in chapter 6 for CSF creation in the departmental/functional working group meeting. Let us imagine you end up with the following list of CSFs:

1. We must know our current environmental performance levels as a baseline for improvement.
2. We need to understand the corporate environmental policy to ensure that we set relevant objectives and targets.
3. We need to have well-motivated staff to achieve the new environmental goals.
4. We must provide appropriate training to ensure that the correct skills are in place.
5. We need to have a programme to make effective use of resources.
6. We must communicate our environmental objectives and targets to our suppliers and customers.
7. We need to integrate environmental performance criteria into our day-to-day operational systems.
8. We must have clearly defined roles and responsibilities to achieve the environmental targets.

Now, list the major activities of the department/function and analyse them against the environmental CSFs. Each activity is described using a verb and a noun, e.g. measure emissions; educate staff; audit systems; review processes; monitor complaints; practise emergency response; recognise achievement. Each activity should have an identified owner in the department whose job it is to ensure that it gets done. The activity should have measurement criteria attached so that you know how well it is being done.

Draw up a chart, similar to the one in Fig. 16.1, to show the interaction of the activities with the environmental CSFs. Then ask the group to identify which of the activities needs to be performed particularly well to achieve the CSFs. Some of the activities will score heavily against more than one CSF. For example, 'measure emissions' will need to be done well to achieve CSFs 1, 5, 6, 7 and 8. The number of crosses against each activity in the chart will give you an indication of its priority. From this analysis you can see that measuring emissions, monitoring legislation and staff training are a high priority. Your list of departmental activities will be longer than the example in Fig. 16.1 so try to focus on the major activities rather than the minutiae.

CSFs	1	2	3	4	5	6	7	8
Activities								
measure emissions	X				X	X	X	X
train staff			X	X		X	X	X
monitor complaints	X					X	X	
control plant	X		X			X		
process products	X							
monitor legislation	X			X		X	X	X

Fig. 16.1 Environmental CSF/activity matrix

You then should ask the question in reverse: 'Have we got in place all the activities necessary to achieve the CSF?' In the example there are no activities supporting the need to understand the corporate goals and policy. So, if it did not exist, the activity of 'monitor corporate direction' would need to be created, given an owner and some measurement criteria.

One further thought, you know what critical factors are necessary to achieve the environmental mission for the department and you know which activities are crucial to ensure that the factors are met. Now check with the group how well they think the activities are being done? If you have no formal measurement ask them to rate the activity against:

A Excellent
B Good
C Fair
D Poor
E Not done at all

This rating allows you to check where resources should be focused. If a critical activity is rated as E, it should receive a higher resource priority.

Planning and documentation

For each of the critical activities identified you must establish the standards of management control you require and document how they are to be achieved in a documented procedure. It helps to map out the process steps in graphic format as this allows you to see where instructions may be needed to assure compliance. The IBM environmental master plan procedure extract shows a map of the process, which is supported by more detailed work instructions at each step.

Each work instruction should, wherever possible, use the standards already within the management system. The goal of integration with existing systems will not be attained if special environmental instructions have to be considered at every step in the process.

CHECKLIST

- *Have you identified the relevant functions, activities and processes which affect the environment?*
- *Have you put in place control procedures for those relevant activities?*
  - *operating instructions where the absence of such instructions could result in failure to meet the requirement*
  - *procurement policies, practices and procedures for contracted activities*
  - *monitoring and control of waste streams, effluent and discharges*
  - *approval processes for plans and equipment investment*
  - *performance criteria documented for the key activities*

COMMUNICATION HINTS

- The presentation of operating instructions and performance criteria must be clear and readily understandable. The graphic mapping of a process may help to explain the process steps more clearly than a written text form.
- Operating instructions do not have to be dull – an upper and lower emissions limit may be translated to a red/amber/green visual scoring criteria.
- You can find out if the managers and staff understand the operating instructions and procedures by listening to their complaints and comments.

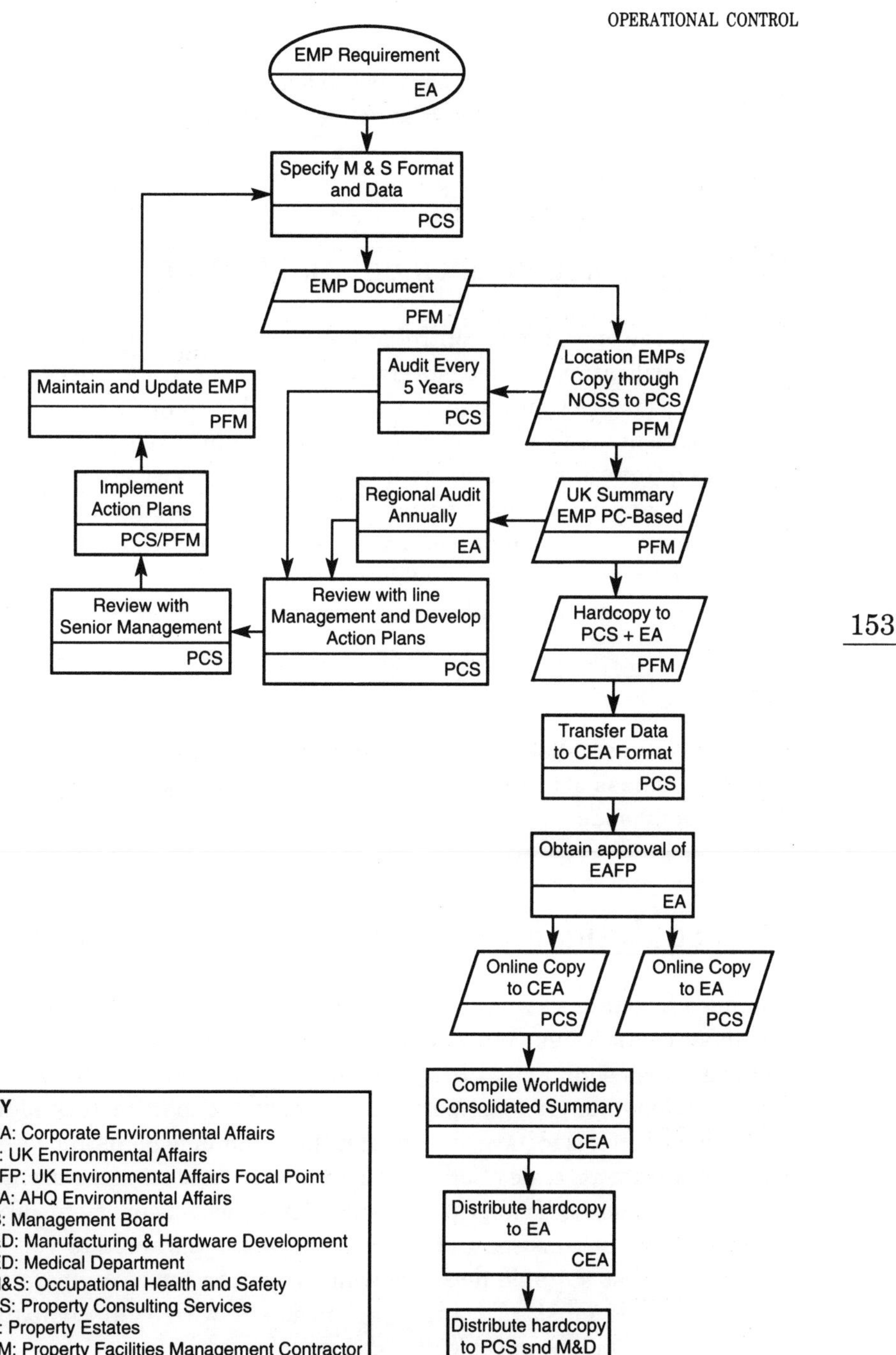

Fig. 16.2 IBM's procedure for environmental master plan control.

- Look for examples of errors or omissions to track weak points in the operating instructions. When you hear people say 'oh yes!' That always goes wrong, always has', you know its time to act.

Verification, measurement and testing

To know if the operational control procedures are working you need an effective verification and measurement system. The system needs to be designed to ensure that it can identify the level of compliance achieved and indicate areas for improvement. Measurements are often designed to advise or inform management of the 'state of play' without regard to the use to which they may be put. They are designed for protection rather than process improvement. Yet operating controls can be complex and the processes subject to fluctuation, so we need a measurement approach that is consistent and comprehensive.

OBJECTIVE

The goal is an established and maintained procedure that will confirm the effectiveness of the operating control procedures and identify areas of non-compliance.

The requirements of a measurement procedure

You need to establish what operations require measuring to show they are under control. Ask yourself what the purpose of measuring is before you begin to design a measuring system. This will help you to focus on the key elements. It is important to know the parameters of the measurement if it is to have any use. Set the acceptable highs and lows of the measurement scale. Set a benchmark or control measurement against which you will gauge performance. Are the measurements likely to be accurate or consistent? Once you know the parameters you can design the most suitable measurement procedure for each operation. The procedures must, of course, be consistent with your company's environmental policy and objectives.

The nature of the measurement will determine the complexity of the system. For example, if the operation requires the recycling of so many items per week or per month, a simple counting procedure will suffice. However, if it is levels of water purity that must be measured, then the procedure is likely to be more complicated. Whatever type of procedure you design it must incorporate a recording and reporting system. Be sure you can trust the measurement records – are they accurately recorded? Establish proper documented procedures where necessary and ensure that the records are maintained and regularly reviewed.

Finally, you will need to check that the testing procedure is accurate. The frequency of checks will depend on the importance of the activity being measured. If the testing method is faulty you will need to validate previous results. Do you have a system in place that can do this? Do you also have a procedure in place to act if the control measurement is not reached or is exceeded? It is pointless to measure, record and report if the data is inaccurate or if the results are not acted upon when necessary. Therefore make sure you have a reporting procedure that generates results that can be used to improve environmental performance effectively.

Measurements techniques

Various techniques can be used to establish the performance measurements. BS7850: Part 2: 1992: Total quality management guide to methods provides some practical techniques that have statistical credibility.

- *Control charts* can monitor the performance process within standard deviation control limits.
- *Histograms* provide a visual presentation of data related to a particular attribute you want to measure.
- *Pareto diagrams* are used to identify the significance of problems that contribute to a non-compliance situation, allowing you to focus on the few issues that cause the majority of the problems.
- *Scatter diagrams* are a simple, graphic technique to illustrate a relationship between two sets of data. The degree of correlation between the data can be understood from the shape of the 'cloud' of dots that results. It can help to identify areas where, because a strong correlation is shown, it is worth developing further measurements.

Examples

Control charts can identify trends. Using control charts a company with significant effluent discharge levels (although always within the upper and lower control limits) was able to reduce progressively the overall levels of discharge and improve the control parameters through: (a) improved filtering systems; and (b) an improved process upstream which reduced the demand on the effluent management systems. A sample chart is shown in Fig. 16.3.

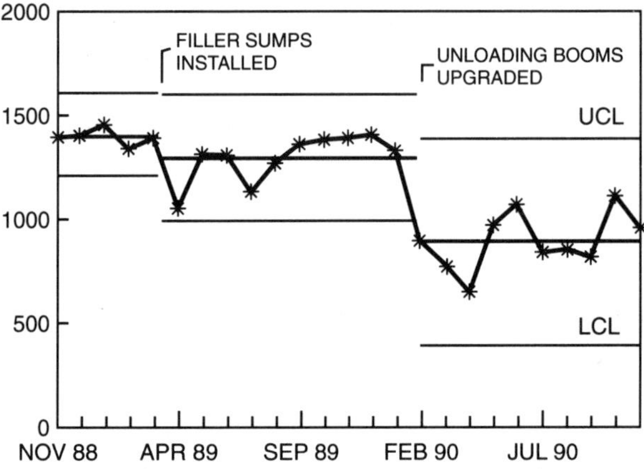

Fig. 16.3 A sample control chart

An example of a pareto diagram is shown in Fig. 16.4. The pareto analysis of Florida Power & Light's hazardous waste violations shows how it can help identify key areas for improvement.

Standard methods of measurement

Tests for process or emission control are essential for adequate control using standard test can help. These provide high levels of confidence and the results can be compared with similar results elsewhere for 'best of breed' comparisons. There are many standard methods of measurement in various industries. The British Standards Institution catalogue contains a range of environmental measurements:

Water: BS6068: various parts: Water quality guidelines on the design of sampling systems and field tests.

BS2690: various parts: Methods of testing water used in industry.

Air: BS1747: various parts: Methods of measurement of air pollution.

BS1756: various parts: Methods of sampling and analysing flue gasses.

BS3405: 1983: Methods of measurement of particulant emissions including grit and dust.

BS6069: various parts: Characterisation of air quality.

Noise: BS4142: 1990: Methods for rating industrial noise affecting mixed residential and industrial areas.

BS7445: various parts: Description and measurement of environmental noise.

Land: DD175: Code of practice for the identification of potentially contaminated land and its investigation.

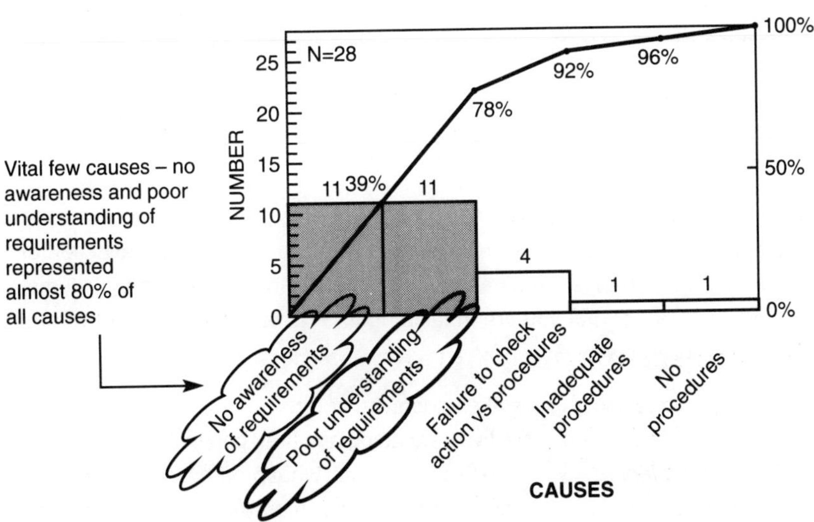

Fig. 16.4 An example of a pareto diagram: causes of Florida Power & Light's hazardous waste violations in 1985

CHECKLIST

- *Have you identified the measurements to be made, their accuracy and control limits?*
- *Have you identified what you want measured and when?*
- *Have you checked these are consistent with the objectives and targets?*
- *Have you identified the measurement procedures, reporting and recording methods?*
- *Have you identified what will happen when control limits are exceeded?*
- *Is the testing equipment kept calibrated and records kept?*
- *Have you a system to re-examine the validity of earlier tests if control limits are exceeded or you find equipment is out of calibration?*

COMMUNICATION HINTS

- Measurements need to be simple and understandable. That is why graphical methods succeed so well – a picture says a thousand words.
- Always try to understand the learning style of the recipient of the information and present in a style that suits them: statistical data for the reflector, trend analysis for the theorist, predictive information for the pragmatist, and graphical illustrations for the activist.
- Keep it simple. A plethora of measurements can be confusing and sometimes contradictory. It is better to aim at a small number of key measurements that all agree.
- Track movement rigorously and show progress and achievement honestly. Be prepared to live with the wrong results if they are an accurate reflection of the reality. Don't change the measurement; change the process, the systems, the product. That is what you are measuring for – to tell you when and where you should be improving.
- Be prepared to show your stakeholders the progress:
  Internal audiences – how well you are doing and their part in it.
  External audiences – what the targets are and what progress you are making.
  All audiences – new opportunities for improvement and higher environmental performance standards.

Non-compliance and corrective action

The expression non-compliance refers to occurrences where environmental performance falls outside the specified requirements. This will be identified by the measurement or verification procedures, the follow-up action to correct the problem is essential for continued confidence in the management system.

ROOT CAUSE ANALYSIS

Non-compliance items must be analysed to establish the cause of the problem in a systematic and structured way to demonstrate a link between the proposed corrective action and the problem. This structured problem solving methodology is sometimes called root cause analysis.

The methodology identifies five stages:

Diagnoses:

1. Identification of the symptoms and problem definition.
2. Cause analysis.
3. Solution analysis and solution criteria

Remedy

4. Solution proposal.
5. Implementation and review.

Note that the solution implementation follows a great deal of analysis to ensure that it accurately fits the underlying problem.

Each of the stages looks at specific aspects of problem solving and there are useful quality tools and techniques that can be used to assist problem analysis.

Problem definition and analysis looks at the symptoms to understand what happened: where, when, how and who is involved. It sets ownership on problem solving and can hypothesise likely causes for further investigation. The output is a more precise problem definition. Useful techniques include data collection, measurements, process analysis, pareto charts, statistical quality control and brainstorming.

Cause analysis develops a set of cause and effect hypotheses and tests the probable ones to identify the root causes to be addressed. Useful techniques include fishbone charts (an example of which is shown in Figure 16.5) and data analysis – an analysis technique that allows a brainstorm to focus on various elements that may cause the problem.

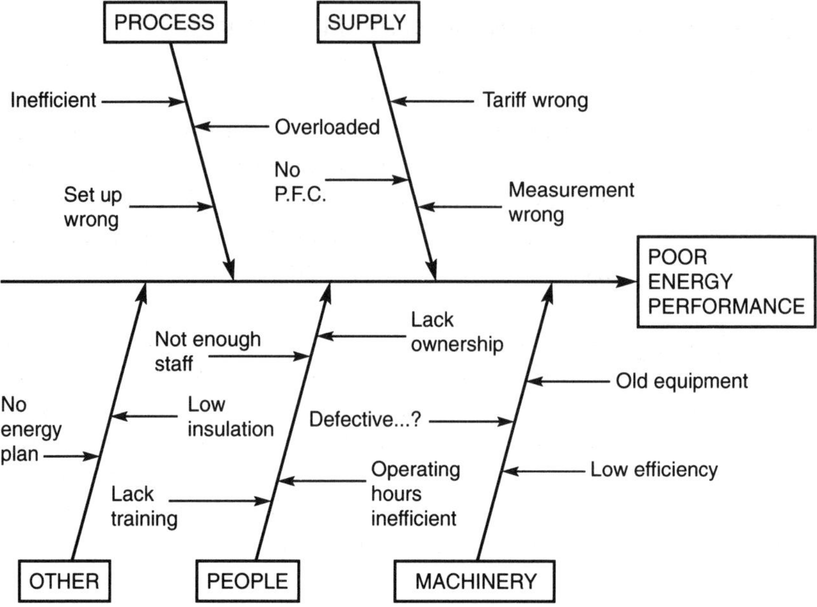

Fig. 16.5 A sample fishbone chart

Solution analysis and solution criteria development look at the results to be achieved by the solution, as a result of the cause analysis, in order to develop a checklist against which to measure possible solutions.

Solution proposal generates a number of ideas for assessment against the solution criteria. Useful techniques include brainstorm, solution impact analysis (reverse fishbone) and cost benefit analysis.

Implementation and review develops a detailed action plan and puts in place the solution that best meets the solution criteria, measuring the impact on the problem. Useful techniques include statistical quality control to assess effectiveness.

Example

The structured approach. A director perceived a communications problem in his department. Messages were not getting through and staff were demotivated.

Step 1 analysed what exactly was wrong with the communications. In this company communications up and down the management line were measured every two years in an opinion survey. By studying these data the project team were able to go back to the director with a revised problem statement: 'There is a communications problem in the department, but at the level between management and staff, the communications between managers is satisfactory. The target should be to raise manager/staff communications to satisfaction levels equal to those between managers, 80 per cent from a current 56 per cent'.

Step 2 involved a detailed local survey to understand why staff rated their communications with management so poorly. A study of the responses showed that whereas messages were getting out to the staff, the timing and attention managers gave to disseminating information was very patchy, and little was done to respond to issues raised by staff. The expanded problem statement then focused on the need to improve the consistency of communication and so that managers responded to the issues raised and passed them up the line.

Step 3 involved looking at what changes in the management communications system might lead to a resolution of the problems. This involved considering all sorts of ideas from using videos, audio-tapes and newsletters, to special 'communication' meetings. The solution that best met the criteria was to improve the frequency and structure of the monthly departmental meetings as a means of communication. Improved agendas and the formal elevation of issues for management review were agreed, together with a more formal senior management review of the frequency of departmental meetings and issues raised up the line.

Step 4 involved implementing the proposed changes in the departmental meetings at every level in the organisation.

Step 5 was a supplementary survey to measure the impact of the changes. Later, the two-yearly full survey showed a sustained improvement in manager/staff communications.

CHECKLIST

- *Have you a procedure for identifying non-conformance through the operational control procedures?*
- *Is there a structural approach to solving problems identified by the operational control procedures?*
- *Does each phase of the problem solving approach have clearly defined start and stop points to enable progress to be tracked?*
- *Have you a training programme in place to train people in problem solving?*

17

Records and record management

The purpose of the requirement is to provide an audit trail to demonstrate to yourself and any assessor the status of the environmental management system and the environmental performance of the organisation. Records are evidence of what has been achieved, the assessor will ask you to show him or her the documented evidence – it is all he or she will believe.

It does not mean that you record everything the organisation does. Keeping records costs money and you should not design your system to keep more than you need, but you must maintain all that is necessary. It should be focused on those areas that are significant and relevant to the main activities and environmental issues of the organisation.

The system of records will cover a wide range of topics to provide the necessary evidence of compliance, i.e. the records required by:

- management;
- legislation;
- the Standard; and
- the Eco-Management and audit Regulation.

OBJECTIVE

The goal is an established and maintained set of records to demonstrate compliance with the BS7750 requirements. The records should also show the extent to which the programme to achieve the environmental objectives and targets has been successful.

The requirements of a records management system

There needs to be an established and maintained procedure for the management of records, from identification to storage and disposal. The records will include information on procurement, audits, reviews and training. They must be legible and identifiable so that they can be related to the activity, product or service to which they refer. Retention times must be established and recorded, and they must be both protected and retrievable during the storage period. The policies on access within the organisation and to outside interested parties must also be established and followed.

The records need to cover all aspects of the system and the environmental performance. Together they must paint an accurate picture of the whole organisation, i.e. no gaps or overlaps. They need to be collated and kept where they are likely to be needed so they will be dispersed throughout the organisation, with local managers having responsibility for local maintenance.

Establishing a records management system

The departmental environmental management system together with the co-ordinating environmental management manual, will provide the requirements of the records system. At the department level you have the identified key measurements to be noted. The environmental management manual provides the overview of key activities and the interrelationships of records, and signposts the assessor along the audit trail to the other documentation required to demonstrate compliance. What is required here is a co-ordinating set of records of management procedures that will guide managers on what should be kept and for how long. This is useful as many managers keep records far longer than is necessary and yet may not have access to a key piece of information when it is really needed.

The records management system is a documented procedure that should identify the main areas of a business and the types of records that are likely to be generated as a result of business activities, allocate the responsibility for each type of record and specify the retention period. Knowing how long and how accessible the documentation needs to be allows the owner to define appropriate storage and retrieval criteria. This is important because for many records related to environmental issues storage times are lengthy. For example, under IPC and APC some emissions not only require continuous monitoring of performance, but the records must also be kept for up to four years, and the information created when classifying substances must be kept for up to three years after the date on which the substance was supplied.

Records need not be piles of paper and large, heavy storage racks. There are many ways of keeping records without excessive paperwork. Consider the use of electronic storage of electronically generated material in long-term databanks as these do not clog-up current, active systems. There is also the use of microfilm and now CD storage and archive systems can 'read' a document and store. Beware however that you only store appropriate materials in these ways. Some legal requirements in contracts require the original documentation to be kept.

What records should be kept?

LEGISLATION

- IPC and APC requirements:
  Emissions, including record of monitoring;
  Discharges, including to surface waters;
  Consents, for processes and activities;
  Licences, for management of wastes;
  COSHH records on substances and assessments;
  Health and Safety reports, especially of accidents and injuries; and
  Management controls that are relevant to environmental issues.
- Planning consents and related environmental assessment records.

BS7750

BS7750 has a list of documentation that will lead to record management requirements:

- Policy statement;
- Responsibilities, authority and interrelationships;

- Verification procedures and records;
- Communication and training procedures and records;
- Register of regulations procedures;
- Communications records;
- Effects evaluation procedures and register of
  - emissions;
  - discharges;
  - wastes;
  - contaminated land;
  - energy and resource use;
  - physical impacts, including noise; and
  - eco-system impacts;
- Considerations for abnormal incidents and accidents;
- Objectives and targets procedures and commitments;
- Environmental Programme including:
  - objectives and targets;
  - projects; and
    new developments;
- Environmental management manual;
- Emergency plans;
- Document control procedures;
- Controls for:
  - management responsibilities;
  - work instructions;
  - process procedures;
  - process performance monitoring;
  - management approvals; and
  - performance criteria;
- Non-compliance and corrective action for:
  - responsibilities;
  - procedures;
  - plans;
  - preventive actions; and
  - procedure changes;
- Records procedures and policies;
- Audit procedures and plans, including;
  - protocols; and
  - reporting;
- Review records.

Examples

Figure 17.1 is an extract from Gleaner's environmental management manual. It describes the procedures for maintaining management records to demonstrate compliance with Gleaner's environmental management system.

CHECKLIST

- *Is your records management system comprehensive?*
- *Is there an audit trail? Can you find your way around the system?*
- *Are the records clearly laid out and readable?*
- *Is there linkage between the co-ordinating document and the departmental records?*
- *Are the records logical in date and process order?*

COMMUNICATION HINTS

- Records are often regarded as the 'Cinderella' part of the system that follows all the other, more important activities. But when the assessor visits it is your records of the management system that will bear the closest scrutiny to assess your compliance. Keep it simple and systematic.
- Readability should be paramount. Imagine that all the records will be subject to public scrutiny (many will be, of course, through public registers).
- Only the necessary critical activity measurements should be passed up to senior management. They will want to know: what topics are important? Where are we now? Where should we be? What is the long-term outlook? Are there any abnormal things we should know?
- Have a special form for highlighting incidents and non-conformity records. Use a red paper to highlight the importance of such pieces of information.

ENVIRONMENTAL MANAGEMENT MANUAL

Gleaner OIL AND GAS

Page: 19
of: 26

GLEANER OILS LTD•MILNFIELD•ELGIN•MORAYSHIRE IV30 IUZ•TEL 0343-547977•TLX 4573205

REVISION	AMENDMENT	PREPARED BY	DATE	APPROVED BY	DATE
00	00	A. Buchanan	09/11/92		16/11/92

4.9 ENVIRONMENTAL MANAGEMENT RECORDS

Section 7 lists the records used to demonstrate compliance with the requirements of the environmental management system. Additional records may be identified by operational procedures manuals.

All staff shall ensure that records under their responsibility are legible, completed correctly and handled/stored to prevent deterioration.

Records shall be retained for the period specified in section 7 after which they shall be reviewed by management. The review shall determine whether they shall be:

destroyed

retained for a further specified period,

archived by microfiche or similar (originals are destroyed).

Records which have been reviewed will be clearly marked or labelled to indicate their disposition.

The availability of records, identified by this manual and operational manuals, to personnel within the company and to interested third parties shall be determined by the Managing Director.

Fig. 17.1 Extract from Gleaner's environmental management manual

Gleaner OIL AND GAS

ENVIRONMENTAL MANAGEMENT MANUAL

Page: 26
of: 26

GLEANER OILS LTD•MILNFIELD•ELGIN•MORAYSHIRE IV30 IUZ•TEL 0343-547977•TLX 4573205

REVISION	AMENDMENT	PREPARED BY	DATE	APPROVED BY	DATE
00	00	A. Buchanan	09/11/92		16/11/92

7 ENVIRONMENTAL MANAGEMENT SYSTEM RECORDS

Doc ID	Title	Location	Retention Period
Q01	Document Master List	Admin Manager	3
Q02	Distribution List	Admin Manager	3
Q03	Transmittal Form	Admin Manager	3
Q04	Purchase Order	Admin Manager	3
Q08	Final Test/Inspection of Nonconforming Product	All Depots	3
Q10	Quarantine Report	All Depots	3
Q11	Customer Complaint Log	Head Office (Elgin)	3
Q12	Measurement Equipment Register	QA Coordinator	3
Q13	Calibration Record	QA Coordinator	3
Q14	Customer Complaint Form	All Depots	3
Q15	Corrective Action Request	QA Coordinator	3
Q16	Audit Reports	QA Coordinator	3
	Environmental management system review meeting minutes	Managing Director	3

Fig. 17.1 contd.

18

Environmental management system audits

The purpose of the requirement is to establish a regular and systematic evaluation of the environmental management system and the related environmental performance to ensure that these comply with BS7750 and are effectively implemented. This is a form of environmental audit but with a specific focus on the EMS. BS7750 and the proposed Eco-management audit Regulation draw parallels with BS5750, EN29000 and ISO9000 Quality systems, and the related audit protocols described in BS7229, EN45000 and ISO10,011: Guide to quality systems audit. The practices, protocols and procedures for an EMS audit are therefore similar to those for a quality systems audit. The same care and attention to scope and the team selection, the same structured approach to information gathering and evaluating the findings, and the same care in identifying non-conformities in reporting are needed. At the conclusion of the EMS audit, the person responsible for the area or activity audited will have a clear indication of the completeness and effectiveness of the environmental management systems in meeting the standard requirements and environmental performance to plan.

This last point can be cause for discussion. It is sometimes assumed that the environmental management system audit is only concerned with the completeness of the environmental management system and not the environmental performance. However, environmental management system audits are set up to determine whether the activities and the results comply with the specified requirements. How else do you know whether the environmental management system, if assessed to be complete, is actually effective? Effectiveness can only be verified by looking at the environmental results (the performance) and assessing whether they meet the policy, objectives and targets.

OBJECTIVE

The goal is an established and maintained set of procedures to enable audits to be carried out.

The auditors

Understanding that EMS auditors will be looking at environmental performance helps to identify what skills will be required by the audit team. Those familiar with quality system auditing may feel that they are competent to assess any quality system – whether for products, services, environmental management or health and safety systems compliance. Those possessing industry-specific knowledge may feel that is sufficient qualification for an EMS auditor. After all, an industry expert would be able to identify whether a company's environmental policy omits a specific industry issue or whether or not the objectives and targets that are set in the EMS meet the legal requirements for BATNEEC or industry practice. Those with an expertise in environmental issues, an essential requirement for an EMS auditor, may feel competent to assess an EMS.

All of these skills are important but each is insufficient on its own. An EMS auditor must have an appropriate mix of auditing and industry-specific skills and be an expert on environmental issues. It is highly unlikely that one person will possess all these attributes (although it sometimes happens) so usually a team of professionals will work together when auditing an EMS. In large organisations the relevant skills may be available in-house, or they may have to be procured from outside companies. In-house auditors must be independent of the department or function they are auditing.

An integrated audit?

Given that the EMS is an integrated part of the management system, why do you need a separate audit procedure? Why not just extend the BS5750 audit procedure?

This is a possible and desirable option for many companies. It has the benefit of a single audit activity and avoids the duplication of costs and resources. However, it is only a viable option if your audit team has the correct mixture of skills to examine the EMS elements of the overall management system, and if your EMS is completely and effectively integrated into the overall management system. For most organisations compliance to quality management requirements affects the purchaser relationship whereas compliance to environmental management requirements affects relationships with legislative bodies, industry watchdogs, local communities, suppliers, purchasers and many more. For many organisations, therefore, the EMS audit will be a separate activity.

The audit procedure

It will help to define the outline of the procedure. Here the method is not a meeting or a workshop, but a suggested form of protocol that should be followed. This may be used in a stand alone audit of the environmental management system, or in a guide to your existing audit function to enable auditors to include environmental management system compliance with the other audit activities. Remember that the thread of the EMS must be woven throughout the overall management system.

The audits are to establish whether or not the EMS activities conform to the environmental programme and are carried out effectively, and to establish the effectiveness of the EMS in fulfilling the organisation's environmental policy. It is more than just the existence of system elements in line with the Standard. It is a test of the system's effectiveness in translating policy into improving performance. To test this, an audit plan is required to cover seven factors:

1. The specific activities and areas to be assessed, including:
   * the organisational structure, roles and responsibilities;
   * the procedures to operate and administer the activities;
   * the activities and processes in the work area;
   * the operating procedures and records; and
   * the environmental performance.
2. The schedule for audit activity, audits being established on the basis of the significance of the activity and the result of previous audits.
3. Definitions of who is responsible for the audit activity in each area.
4. Definitions of the criteria for staff who carry out audits. Auditors must be:
   * independent from the areas being audited;
   * have some expertise in the relevant discipline; and be
   * supported by specialists wherever necessary.
5. The protocol for conducting the audit, i.e. the order of events, collection of evidence and recording of findings.

6. The procedure for reporting the audit findings to those who are responsible for the audit area or activity and identifying those who are responsible for taking action on the reported deficiencies. The report should include:

   * EMS conformity or non-conformity with requirements;
   * EMS effectiveness in meeting objectives and targets;
   * follow-up of previous audit findings; and
   * conclusions and recommendations.

7. The procedures for publishing the audit findings.

The key to success in establishing an EMS audit plan is to nominate the owner of the activity and provide them with the management tools to implement the plans and procedures. From the departmental EMS documentation you will have a plan of audit activity. This is the requirement that has to be met. That plan will also provide information on the skills required to carry out the audit successfully.

SELECTING THE AUDIT TEAM

The audit programme manager must be independent of the area being audited. In large organisations like IBM or Shell, for example, there is position dedicated to auditing activities, but in smaller organisations it will be one of several responsibilities for an individual. In this case, one successful way to approach the audit is that function A audits function B, which audits function C which audits function A. The protocols and procedures must be common (see below). The audit activity can also be treated as a purchased service from an outside agency, consultant or assessor.

From knowledge of the area/activity to be assessed it is possible to draw up auditor criteria, and then establish a pool of suitably qualified people in the organisation to draw on for the programme. You will need to ensure that the common protocols are understood by all the auditors you propose to use. So spend time reviewing these in a joint training session. As the audit programme progresses you will need to review auditor performance to ensure confidence in the audit results.

Each audit team will have a *lead auditor*, a senior person responsible for a particular assessment and the *auditors*, the people making the assessments. The *programme manager* is responsible for the overall audit programme. There may occasionally be a sponsor of the audit other than the programme manager or the *auditee*, the person responsible for the area being assessed, and this third party is called the *client*. Examples of clients may be an organisation's customer or a prospective purchaser.

CHECKLIST: EMS audit management considerations

- *Is there an internal audit capability?*
  You must have the capacity to audit the EMS system and the environmental performance of the organisation.
- *What are the EMS standards you are auditing against?*
  You must have a standard against which to assess compliance. 'We have an EMS that meets the requirements of BS7750/Eco-Management and audit Regulation/BACMI code of practice/Responsible Care guidelines'.
- *Have you identified an audit programme manager?*
  Someone with necessary knowledge of EMS audit practices and procedures.

- *Have you identified the auditor skills you require?*
  They must be relevant to the requirements of the audit programme, activities and processes.
- *Do you have a pool of qualified auditors?*
  They must be appropriate to: the type of organisation, have the relevant regulatory knowledge, personal skills, language skills, be independent.
- *Have you established a programme to ensure consistency in the audit?*
  You must train staff to ensure a common approach and mix and match teams so that consistency develops.
- *Have you a mechanism for evaluating the performance of the audit team?*
  You must ensure that the audits are appropriately carried out through some form of audit assessment.

THE KEY STEPS IN THE EMS AUDIT

Figure 18.1 indicates the main steps in the audit process to be considered by the audit programme manager.

Scope: Establish the range or boundaries of the audit activity: where, what and when. There are benefits if the auditee and lead auditor can discuss and agree.

Standards: Establish the standards or the criteria that the assessment will use to seek evidence of compliance.

THINKING

- Scope
- Standards
- Select lead auditor
- Scan material

PLANNING

- Select team
- Plan audit
- Assign auditors
- Establish documents

DOING

- Opening meeting
- Accumulate evidence
- Review evidence
- Record findings

REVIEWING

- Draft report
- Review
- Closing meeting
- Final report

Fig. 18.1 The main steps in the EMS audit process

Select lead auditor: Choose the lead auditor and brief him or her on the scope and criteria of the audit.
Scan material: Review the scope to obtain information for selecting the team. Review the documented EMS for completeness and as an aid to planning.
Select team: In the light of the audit scope and EMS review, select the rest of the team.
Plan audit: Establish the areas and times to carry out the audit.
Assign auditors: Allocate the duties of the audit team.
Establish documents: Establish the assessment methods and working documents. Agree the plan with the auditee.
Opening meeting: Hold an opening meeting with the auditee, his or her management team and the audit team. Explain the scope, plan and method of the audit and set the time of the closing meeting.
Accumulate evidence: Collect the evidence by the methods planned. Be prepared to follow an audit trail where evidence indicates a non-compliance.
Review evidence and record findings: Establish the areas of non-compliance. These may be within the system, aspects of the performance or any aspect within the scope of the audit.
Draft report: Document the findings in a clear and concise manner, identifying non-compliant items with supporting evidence.

Review: Analyse the findings with the auditee and obtain acknowlegement of the non-compliant items.

Closing meeting: Hold a minuted meeting with the auditors and auditee management teams. Ensure that they understand and agree with the results of the audit and its recommendations.

Final report: Prepare the final report and distribute to the manager responsible for the area, his manager and the Environmental programme manager. Note that the auditee is then responsible for deciding on the necessary corrective action and implementation.

Examples

The Union Carbide audit programme includes compliance audits, management systems reviews and other forms of performance assessment. The objective is to provide independent assessment of line manager performance for compliance with legal, internal standards and management systems that assure continued compliance.

In assessing audit results, a classification is used for the findings (called exceptions and observations) which form the basis for the ongoing environmental improvement plan. Exceptions are rated as 'imminent' – demands immediate attention; 'priority' – has a potential for serious adverse effects; or 'other'. Each functional area is then viewed overall, including the exceptions and compliance factors. Departments may be rated M = meets compliance requirements; SM = substantially meets; GM = generally meets; RSI = requires substantial improvement to meet requirements. For an audit of a function to obtain a 'meets' classification, at least 75 per cent of the departments assessed must be rated M with no part rated GM or lower.

The NEC system (Fig. 18.2) shows the relations between the consultation arm of the business which advises and guides on the business activities, standards and procedures and the plant/business division and departmental teams which implement action and the audit, including self-inspection at business division level. NEC have different categories of audit depending on the type of activity and its potential environmental impact. For production companies, types 1, 2 and 3 cover special patrol (inspection), interview or presentation audit activity. For service and software activities the audit categories are simplified to types 4 and 5 – patrol and document-check type audits.

Audit items include management systems, plan-performance,

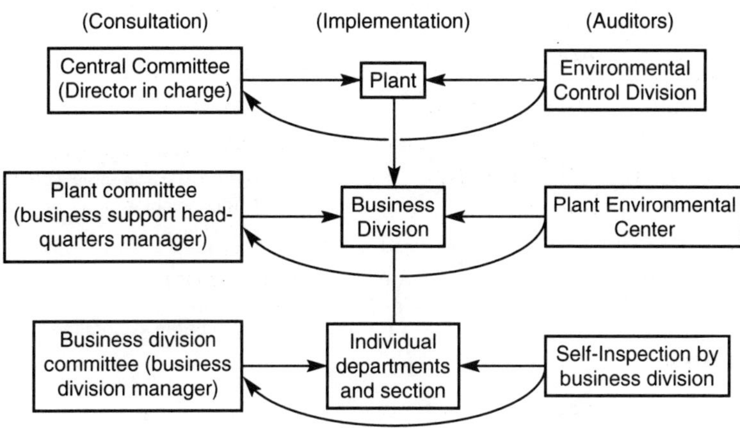

Fig. 18.2 Extract from Union Carbide's Audit Classification Programme

technologies, relationships with residents and supporting co-operative companies (what we might call suppliers, but note how the term reflects the perceived role of suppliers in the procurement chain!). Audit results are shown here against a scoring wheel that shows where compliance exceeds the needs (outside the circle) and where it falls short (inside the circle) and by how much. In the example shown, Fig. 18.3, one might expect action areas to include technologies, awareness and resident relations.

Audit frequency

The frequency of auditing the EMS will depend upon the factors of environmental performance risk. Areas of high environmental risk, complex processes and activities will be audited more frequently than administrative or support functions. In addition, consideration must be made of the result of previous audits which may indicate a need for an assessment of parts of the system where problems and significant non-conformance is found.

The whole organisation should complete an audit cycle within a three year period to meet the requirement of the Eco-management and audit regulation. Some areas will be assessed annually if they meet the criteria indicated, where the nature and scale of activities demands

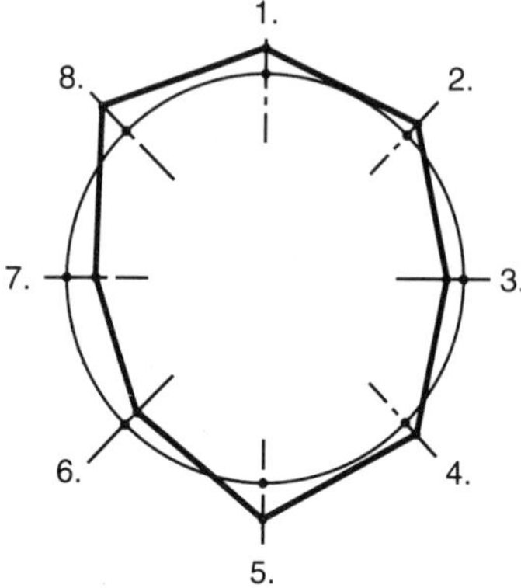

Fig. 18.3 The NEC audit result wheel

a more regular scrutiny of the environmental management system performance.

Audit documentation

The records of audit findings, plans, non-conformance data and final reports form part of the environmental records management system. These must be retained to provide an adequate audit trail for external assessment and follow-up action by the manager responsible for the area assessed.

CHECKLIST

- *Do you have a documented EMS audit procedure?*
- *Do the procedures cover:*
  - *the environmental management manual review?*
  - *activity review against the programme?*
  - *assessment criteria to establish effectiveness?*
  - *planning protocols?*

- *Do the audit planning procedures include:*
  - *organisation, procedures, activities, documents and environmental performance?*
  - *frequency of audits?*
  - *responsibilities defined at all levels?*
  - *personnel and skill requirements?*
  - *protocol for logging non-compliances?*
  - *measures for reporting?*
  - *publishing plans?*

- *Do the protocols cover:*
  - *the scope of the assessment?*
  - *the assessment criteria?*
  - *the standards?*
  - *roles and responsibilities?*
  - *team selection?*
  - *outline planning?*
  - *operating documents?*
  - *the opening meeting?*
  - *evidence gathering?*
  - *recording the findings?*
  - *reporting the findings*
  - *the closing meeting?*

COMMUNICATION HINTS

- The role of audit is about as popular in some businesses as the VAT inspector. The perception exists that the auditor is 'someone from Head Office come to catch us out'. Try to dispel this perception by using your communications system to clarify that the auditor's role is to facilitate improvement through objective assessment. At each phase ensure that the presentation of the audit activity is consistent with the concept of a healthy exploration of strengths as well as weaknesses, opportunities and threats.

  Thinking: Communicate with the management of the area being audited early on so that they feel involved in the scope and planning of the audit and the decision-making. Explore fully the process and the outputs that will be generated to allay any fears of witch-hunt management.

  Planning: Ensure that all those likely to be approached by the auditors are aware of the audit, its purpose and its approach. Aim at 'no surprises'.

  Doing: Skilled auditors will always use an appropriate approach to assessments but the 'Show me . . .' question can often elicit responses like, 'I am much too busy. See my subordinate' or even a demonstration of pride if it is going well. The auditors' style should be professional and open. A non-compliance, when identified, should be documented at the time and acknowledged by the departmental representatives' signature.

Reviewing: The draft report review is an opportunity to ensure that the local management are aware of and agree that the audit report contents are factually accurate. It provides an opportunity for them to prepare the outlines of a planned response for the closing meeting.

The presentation of the meeting should begin with thanks for the co-operation that will have been received, a summary of the overall findings, with reference to specifics if that is required, and a statement as to the auditee's status against the requirements of the Standard. Recommendations for actions and priorities should conclude the presentation. You must allow some time for discussion to clear any misunderstandings and ensure that the recommendations are accepted.

- The audit is an evaluation of the environmental management systems' performance, not the managers' performance. The report must therefore always be an accurate, objective view of what is found, not a performance appraisal of the staff involved.

19

Management reviews

The purpose of the requirement is to ensure that senior managers responsible for the organisation's environmental management system have the opportunity to assess the overall performance and the need to adapt any of its components parts, from policy through to audit. For many organisations the review is an opportunity to promote publicly their environmental contribution.

OBJECTIVE

The goal is a report which summarises the status of the organisation's environmental management system and current environmental performance, reviews external and internal pressures for change and agrees an action plan for change.

The management review meeting

The key to reviewing the environmental management system is the regular management meeting that reviews the overall position. The meeting should include a report from the environmental programmes manager. The report should comprise the following:

- the results of audits and assessments;
- the progress of improvement plans and programmes;
- the actions taken on non-compliances;
- an overview of new and planned legislation;
- the performance of suppliers and partners;
- a review of public environmental issues;
- a summary of the concerns of the local community; and
- new environmental concerns from any area.

The report is planned as a regular, probably annual, agenda item on the management executive meeting. Prior to the meeting you will prepare a summary of the organisation's current status, based on the information from the various functional or departmental assessments, and a review of the progress in improvement plans.

In addition to the report from you, each senior manager or department/functional head should have the opportunity to report for a few minutes on developments, achievements and new challenges in his or her relevant business area. For example, the senior marketing manager might report on recent trends in the market place, what the competition is doing, or new opportunities being researched for 'greener' products with a marketing edge. The operations senior manager might report on new practices and processes that are being reported as BATNEEC or BEO and that need to be considered in the next round of investment plans. Other brief reports might also be made on relevant legislative developments, external community issues, corporate or promotional plans.

Prepare a draft report and circulate this to the environmental steering committee for agreement. The report will be based on the EMS documentation material, audit results and non-compliance action plans. Finalise the report and send it in advance to the executive team members. Prepare a short summary presentation to capture the key elements of the report for the meeting.

A MODEL AGENDA: ENVIRONMENTAL MANAGEMENT REVIEW MEETING

1. Present the current position of the organisation (environmental programmes manager)
2. Review by business areas (business unit managers)
3. Review of regulatory and legislative factors (legal department)
4. Report on current internal development plans (environmental programmes manager)
5. Report on external and community promotion plans (communications manager)
6. Conclusions and recommendations (environmental programmes manager)

The publication requirements

BS7750 compliance requires the publication of environmental policy, objectives and targets, but not the audit results. However, many organisations do publish the audit results and review the information it provides, see examples.

The proposed EC Eco-Mangement and audit Regulation, however, asks for the following information to be included in the public statement:
Name of company
Name and location of the site (the Eco-Management and audit Regulation is site based)
Brief description of the activities at the site (referring to annexed documents if necessary)
(Allows for a standard company document to be used in support of the statement)
Name and address of the accredited environmental verifier who validated the statement attached
Deadline for submission of the next validated environmental statement

The following details must be annexed to the statement:
(a) A brief description of the environmental protection system.
(b) A description of the auditing programme established for the site.
(c) The initial validated environmental statement.
(The statement must include details of:
- the activities concerned;
- the environmental problems raised by these activities;
- an inventory of emissions, of waste generation and of energy and raw material consumption;
- the company's environmental policy, programme and objectives; and
- the company's environmental performance)

Examples

In 1992 IBM published 'IBM and the Environment – A Progress Report', indicating the range of environmental activities and achievements across the corporation. Subjects in the report included environmental impact assessments and the programme for the environmental master plans; health and safety records including lost-time injury rates; pollution prevention – eliminating J-100 air emissions from the East Fishkill plant; Ozone depleting substances – 83 per cent reductions; Chemical releases – a 40 per cent reduction in off-site waste transfers; waste management – 61 per cent recycling at M & D plants; energy manage-

ment – a $32 million saving in 1991; and other national and international initiatives.

DOW Europe's 1992 report covered a profile of the organisation and its commitment to change towards an improved environmental performance. The report set out goals for tomorrow in a number of areas: waste reduction (a 50 per cent commitment); measurement of emissions including fugitive emission issues; groundwater protection, remediation and protection processes; life-cycle analysis as a planning tool; plastics re-valorisation – a recycling strategy; energy conservation; and plans for third-party validation. The report then explored the European results from 28 sites with data on:

- *production tonnes;*
- *energy-related emissions;*
- *halogenated compounds;*
- *waste water;*
- *waste;*
- *energy use;*
- *Chemical Oxygen Demand (COD)*
- *chemical priorities; and*
- *CFCs.*

Detailed information on waste water, air emissions and waste was supplied for all the individual sites.

The Body Shop published The Green Book *in May 1992. It covered a wide range of issues including: a Board statement; and measurements and plans from corporate performance to individual shop targets. It was designed to meet the needs of the proposed EC Eco-audit Regulation public statement. Included in the publication was a verification statement by Arther D. Little, which confirms areas of good and best practice as well as identifying areas of further action to remedy some agreed shortcomings.*

CHECKLIST

- *Is there a regular management review planned?*
- *Does the review cover*
  - *policy?*
  - *environmental management system?*
  - *audit results?*
  - *corrective action plans?*
  - *performance measures?*
  - *legislation?*

- *outside factors?*
- *investment?*

COMMUNICATION HINTS

- Ensure that the results of the audits and plans are agreed before the closing meeting to avoid any contentious issues.
- Publish the results, warts and all, nobody will believe a statement of perfection.
- Tell the truth.
- Focus on the facts.

PART IV

■

Reviewing the implementation of the environmental management system

20

The final report

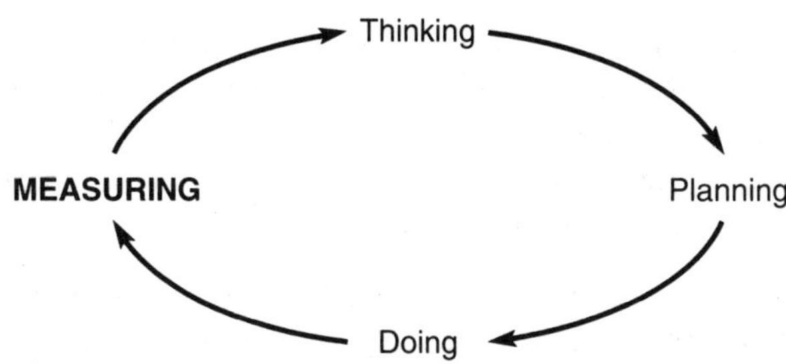
Thinking
MEASURING
Planning
Doing
MEASURING: Reviewing progress to plan and identifying areas for improvement.

Fig. 20.1 The 'measuring' part of the improvement loop

The final section of Part 3; Doing, was the management review of the EMS and related environmental performance. This part of the book is intended to provide an approach to assessing the effectiveness of the project implementation through:

- the final report, and
- a self-assessment questionnaire

OBJECTIVE

To prepare a final report on the implementation of the environmental management system for senior management. Identify its achievements against the original plan and make recommendations on what to think about and plan for in any future activity.

The final report

Your project measurement criteria will have been established at the start of the project, your regular reviews will have kept management appraised of progress to the plan. Now you need a final report. The report will not just comment on the progress of the project; it will also cover the end-product – the integrated EMS. The report should:

- Identify areas where there are still gaps in system performance against the Standard;
- point towards areas where control limits can be tightened to reduce costs;
- indicate where wastes or impacts can be further reduced;
- identify improvement areas where you can now set more challenging targets from your new baseline;
- indicate where further focus on shared values, strategy, structure, staff, skills, systems, or style is needed.

The report should be based on an internal project review of the EMS in place by you and the project team, to give you information on current issues. It should include reference to the original project scope, plan and results. The internal project review can be based on the results of the self-assessment questionnaire (see Chapter 21). The remaining information will be in your project files.

The internal project review

This review will be carried out by you and the project team at regular meetings on completion of the EMS review. All members of the team should be invited to make a short presentation of their views of the project activity in their departments or functions. Each presentation should cover:

- Key points of original plan
- Key points of actual progress
- Highlights – positive lessons learned
- Lowlights – things to be avoided in future
- Recommendations for improvement.

Your presentation should follow the same format as above and include the results from self-assessment audits that you will have encouraged managers to undertake (see Chapter 21).

As the presentations are made, keep track of the key points on a flip chart in front of the project team. At the end of the meeting, review the contents of the charts to agree the key factors to form part of the final report.

After the meeting, prepare a draft report, send this to the project team members for review and comment, and consolidate the comments into a final report.

Establish a review session on the executive management meeting, send out the report ahead of the meeting and prepare a brief 15 to 20 minute presentation on the contents. At the meeting, allow time for the presentation and some discussion on the recommendations for follow-up action.

A self-assessment technique

Self-assessment techniques allow managers to take an objective look at their status against the requirements of the Standard. The usual methods of analysis employed by managers is a questionnaire or checklist that provides a useful indicator for the breadth and depth of the penetration of the environmental management system into the area under consideration.

A questionnaire can be found in Chapter 21, similar in design to that used to assist participants of the BS7750 pilot programme in tracking their progress. It aims to meet the needs of departmental, functional heads or programme managers in establishing where they are in developing and implementing their environmental management systems. The results can be used by managers to focus on the areas of improvement and to identify common areas of weakness across the organisation where specific company-wide actions may be needed.

The chart shown in Fig. 20.2 is a condensed example drawn from the early results from the BS7750 pilot programme. The questionnaire used had questions covering activities from the preliminary review through to the EMS audit and management review. Overall it showed that, even with organisations that have well-established management systems, designed and assessed to meet the requirements of BS5750, the scores against each question averaged just under 1 out of a potential score of 4.

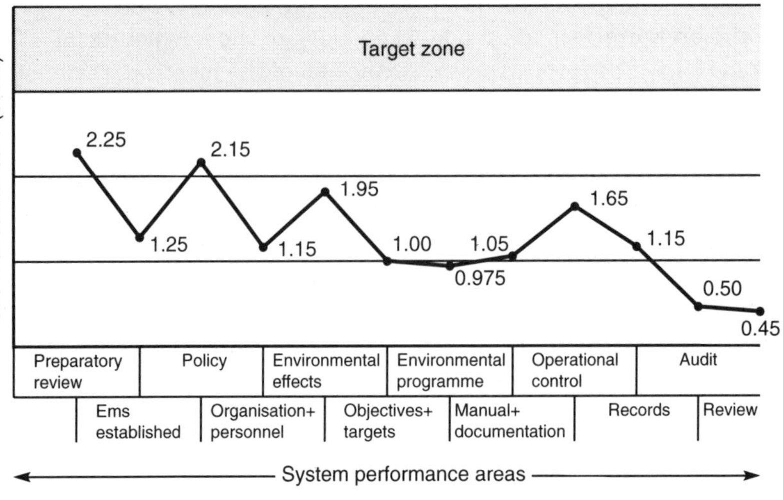

A composite of results from self-assessment questionnaires showed the above trend.

Fig. 20.2 Results of a self-assessment questionnaire

THE RESULTS OF THE BS7750 PILOT PROGRAMME'S SELF-ASSESSMENT QUESTIONNAIRE

Let us look at the results of the pilot programme's self-assessment questionnaire. They provide an illuminating insight of the highlights and lowlights of EMS implementation and comprise a useful learning tool for EMS programme managers.

The consistently highest score was the response to Question 1: Have you carried out an initial review? Nearly a third of all respondents were able to score well here. Scoring almost as high was the answer to Question 3: Have you defined and documented your environmental policy? A similarly positive response was reported on Question 6: Has the organisation appointed a management representative?

These highlights indicated that many of the organisations in the pilot programme had begun to take positive steps towards implementing an EMS. They knew where they stood and had established a policy and owner at high levels to implement the policy. But there were also lowlights. Figure 20.2 shows that scores then fell away across the broad needs of environmental management system implementation. This was confirmed by the lower response to Question 2: Has the organisation adopted and implemented an environmental management system designed to meet the requirements of BS7750? The responses to Questions 7 through to 11, on communications, training, the regulatory requirements register, the views of interested parties and the environmental effects documentation, were similar. The scores for Questions 12 to 16, on the establishment of procedures for setting objectives and targets, the environmental management manual and other documentation, also showed a low response.

The results showed an improvement for Questions 17, 18 and 19 – requirements for management ownership of control, verification, measurement and testing. This is consistent with the BS5750 requirements for such management control, and is therefore perhaps not surprising. Similarly, the improvement in the responses to Question 21 on responsibility and authority for initiating corrective action in the event of non-compliance, is probably related to quality system procedures. The lower response to Question 20 (procedures for maintaining records of verification activities) is consistent with the significantly low responses to Questions 24, 25 and 26 on the establishment of internal environmental audit procedures, audit plans and management reviews.

In general the results provided useful support for participating companies. The fact that the results followed a general trend encouraged companies to focus on the low areas and share ideas on how to improve; their ratings. For example, Texaco's initial response to the questionnaire showed a similar pattern when undertaken by refinery staff. The initial score was 25, but after a few months' work this total had risen to 46, showing significant progress.

For Texaco scores were high in the areas of the initial review, organisation and personnel, environmental effects, documentation and operational control. Lower scores were recorded in the EMS establishment of policy, objectives and targets and the evaluation of effects. Very little was scored in the areas of preparation of the manual, keeping records, environmental management systems audits and environmental management reviews – it is difficult to record audits that have not taken place yet!

The self-assessment questionnaire proved an excellent way of gauging companies' performance in the BS7750 pilot programme. Valuable lessons were learned. It is not the measurements you take that lead to improvement, but rather what you do with the results of the measurements. The pilot programme itself helped the participating companies move forward plans for change in their organisations and performance management. The results provided an excellent opportunity for education.

Using the self-assessment questionnaire

As part of the EMS implementation review procedure, managers should be invited to assess their system design and performance against the self-assessment questionnaire in Chapter 21.

By analysing the results from the summary reports, you can create a chart similar to Fig. 20.2, which shows a 'profile' of the conformance to BS7750 requirements. It will readily indicate those areas where compliance is high and little improvement action is required, and those where compliance is low, indicating that some further action may be required.

21

The self-assessment questionnaire

This is a self-assessment technique for those involved in environmental management system implementation. It will allow you and your management team to check your progress against the requirements of the Standard and identify areas for improvement. The questions are set in a linear scale using two extremes, between 'not yet started' to 'full compliance' with the specified requirements of BS 7750. The questionnaire should be used as a desktop exercise using your best judgement on the status of the EMS implementation programme within your organisation. Some checking may be useful if you are not clear where things stand, but this should be limited. The idea is to complete the questionnaire in a single work-session during a morning or an afternoon.

Example

Q6: Has the organisation appointed a management representative, with defined authority and responsibility, for ensuring an EMS is established and maintained in conformance with the requirements of BS 7750?

Score		
4		Management representative demonstrably effective.
3	X	Management representative in place and having an effect.
2		Management representative appointed, with defined authority and responsibility.
1		Management representative appointed, role not fully developed.
0		Management representative not appointed.

Note: All aspects have to be in place to score highly. An appointed environmental manager is not enough. He or she must have defined roles, comprehensively documented, that includes all the necessary authority and responsibility to implement the programme of work. To score 4 requires demonstrable evidence of effectiveness through impact on the environmental activities.

SCORE: 3 LAST ASSESSMENT: 2

The questionnaire

FUNCTIONAL/DEPARTMENT BEING ASSESSED:

ASSESSOR'S NAME:	DATE OF ASSESSMENT:

Q1: Has an initial environmental review been carried out to establish the current environmental management performance?

4	Initial review carried out in a comprehensive manner across the whole organisation.
3	Partial initial review carried out, sufficient to progress the EMS implementation programme.
2	Initial review commenced in part of the organisation.
1	Little progress made in an initial review.
0	Initial review not established.

Note: All aspects have to be in place to score highly. A comprehensive environmental review that looks at all significant activities in sufficient depth to provide a clear direction for the development of an EMS implementation programme is required. To score 4 requires demonstrable evidence of effectiveness through impact on the environmental activities.

SCORE: LAST ASSESSMENT:

Q2: Has a environmental management system been established as a means of ensuring that the effects of the activities of the

organisation conform to its environmental policy, objectives and targets?

4	EMS fully integrated, documented and demonstrably effective.
3	EMS documented and effective in some areas.
2	Some EMS documentation and instruction, with defined authority and responsibility
1	Some elements of a system exist with limited effectiveness.
0	No discernible system elements exist.

Note: All aspects have to be in place to score highly. An intent to create a system is not enough. A fully documented and effectively implemented system is required to score 4. This would be measured by a completed, independent audit.

SCORE: LAST ASSESSMENT:

Q3: Is the organisation's environmental policy defined, documented and effectively implemented?

4	Policy is relevant and fully integrated into the organisation's management system.
3	Policy is in place but not fully implemented, nor meets all requirements.
2	Policy exists but does not address all the requirements and implementation has not started.
1	Policy exists in draft.
0	No policy exists.

Note: All aspects have to be in place to score highly. A policy must be relevant, understood, implemented and maintained throughout the organisation. It must be publicly available, include a commitment to continual improvement in environmental performance and linked to the setting of environmental objectives and targets.

SCORE: LAST ASSESSMENT:

Q4: Is the responsibility, authority and interrelationships of key

personnel who manage, perform and verify work affecting the environment defined and documented?

4	Responsibility and authority are fully documented and integrated.
3	Responsibility and authority are documented with some integration.
2	Responsibility and authority are allocated but not fully documented.
1	Responsibility and authority are partially identified.
0	No responsibility and authority has been allocated or documented.

Note: All aspects have to be in place to score highly. Responsibility, authority and interrelations must include the authority to provide resources, initiate action, identify and record problems, initiate and implement solutions to environmental problems and to ensure that accidents and incidents are properly controlled and acted upon.

SCORE: LAST ASSESSMENT:

Q5: Are there documented in-house verification requirements, established procedures and adequate resources and are assigned, trained personnel provided for the verification activities?

4	Verification activities fully resourced and effective.
3	Verification activities being planned and resourced.
2	Verification procedures and training being developed.
1	Verification requirements being assessed.
0	Verification requirements not known.

Note: All aspects have to be in place to score highly. Verification requirements must be identified and relevant procedures, resources staff and training put in place to meet the needs identified.

SCORE: LAST ASSESSMENT:

Q6: Is there an appointed management representative, with defined authority and responsibility, for ensuring an EMS is established and maintained in compliance with the requirements of BS7750?

4	Management representative demonstrably effective.
3	Management representative appointed and working.
2	Management representative position established, with defined authority and responsibility.
1	Management representative appointed, role not fully developed.
0	Management representative not appointed.

Note: All aspects have to be in place to score highly. An appointed environmental manager is not enough. He or she must have a defined role, comprehensively documented, that includes all the necessary authority and responsibility to implement the programme of work. To score 4 requires demonstrable evidence of effectiveness through impact on the environmental activities.

SCORE: LAST ASSESSMENT:

Q7: Are communication procedures established and maintained to ensue that employees at all levels in the organisation are: aware of the importance of compliance with environmental policy; the potential effects of their activities, their roles and responsibilities and potential consequences of departure from agreed procedures?

4	Communication procedures demonstrably effective, ownership established.
3	Communication procedures in place and working, awareness established.
2	Communication procedures established.
1	Communication procedures being initiated.
0	Communication procedures not yet developed.

Note: All aspects have to be in place to score highly. A communication programme is not enough. There must be evidence of effective and motivating communication procedures with staff at all levels being aware of the commitment to and impact of environmental performance improvement. A score of 4 suggests a fully and motivational two-way process is demonstrably in place.

SCORE: LAST ASSESSMENT:

Q8: Are there established and maintained procedures for identifying training needs and the implementation of personnel training for all key staff?

4	Training requirement procedures in place, programmes implemented and records maintained.
3	Training requirement procedures understood, some new training implemented.
2	Training requirements procedures being identified, some existing training.
1	Some training procedures exist.
0	No environmental training procedures exist.

Note: All aspects have to be in place to score highly. A set of procedures for identifying environmental training needs to be in place is not enough. It must be appropriate to the roles of the individual and include relevant motivational aspects to ensure commitment and ownership at every level. Appropriate records must be kept to show the extent and effectiveness of the training to score 4.

SCORE: LAST ASSESSMENT:

Q9: Are there established and maintained procedures for recording all legislative, regulatory and other policy requirements pertaining to the environmental aspects of its business?

4	Regulatory record procedures fully established and maintained across all activities.
3	Regulatory record procedures established, in most activities.
2	Regulatory record procedure being initiated but not fully operational.

1	Some regulatory record procedures exist.
0	No regulatory record procedures exist.

Note: All aspects have to be in place to score highly. The resultant records should show evidence of a comprehensive approach to the environmental aspects of activities, products and services, including suppliers and disposal issues. To score 4 requires demonstrable evidence of effectiveness through impact on the activities, products and services.

SCORE: LAST ASSESSMENT:

Q10: Are procedures established and maintained to receive, document and respond to communications from relevant interested parties concerning environmental effects and management?

4	Communication procedures established and demonstrably effective.
3	Communication procedures exist and are working.
2	Communication procedures are partly developed.
1	Some communication procedures initiated.
0	No communication procedures exist.

Note: All aspects have to be in place to score highly. An established set of procedures for receiving, documenting and responding to internal and external communications must include some evidence that cognisance is made of the communications received. To score 4 requires demonstrable evidence of effectiveness through impact on the environmental activities.

SCORE: LAST ASSESSMENT:

Q11: Are there established and maintained procedures for examining and assessing the environmental effects of activities, products and services, and for compiling a register of those identified as significant?

4	Effects evaluation procedures and register established, comprehensive and effective.
3	Effects evaluation procedures and register exists.
2	Effects evaluation procedures and register, being developed.
1	Effects evaluation procedures and register partially initiated.
0	Effects evaluation procedures do not exist.

Note: All aspects have to be in place to score highly. An environmental effects assessment procedure and register must comprehensively address all aspects of the activities, emissions, discharges, wastes, contamination, resource use, impact and other effects. It must include upstream and downstream effects, normal, abnormal and emergency considerations. To score 4 requires demonstrable evidence of effectiveness through impact on the environmental activities.

SCORE: LAST ASSESSMENT:

Q12: Are there procedures established and maintained to specify environmental objectives and targets throughout the organisation?

4	Objectives and target procedures established, maintained and demonstrably effective.
3	Objectives and target procedures established and maintained in many parts of the organisation.
2	Objectives and target procedures being established in some parts of the organisation.
1	Few objectives and target procedures developed.
0	Objectives and target procedures not established.

Note: All aspects have to be in place to score highly. Objectives and targets should demonstrate a comprehensive coverage within the organisation and be relevant to the effects analysis, regulations and interested parties. The commitment to continuous improvement should be quantified. To score 4 requires demonstrable evidence of effectiveness through impact on the environmental activities.

SCORE: LAST ASSESSMENT:

Q13: Is there an established programme to achieve the objectives and targets?

4	Comprehensive programme established and implemented in all parts of the organisation.
3	Programme established in many parts of the organisation.
2	Programme established in parts of the organisation.
1	Programme planned in parts, but not fully developed.
0	No programme exists.

Note: All aspects have to be in place to score highly. The environmental programme should be a series of improvement projects relevant to the key business areas and their objectives and targets. To score 4 requires demonstrable evidence of effectiveness through impact on the environmental activities.

SCORE: LAST ASSESSMENT:

Q14: Is there an established and maintained environmental management manual?

4	Comprehensive integrated manual demonstrably effective.
3	Manual established in many parts of the organisation.
2	Manual exists in parts.
1	Outline manual being prepared.
0	No work on the manual.

Note: All aspects have to be in place to score highly. Having an environmental manual is not enough. It must comprehensively cover policy, objectives, programme, key roles and responsibilities. The interaction of system elements will be described and it will relate to other relevant documentation. It covers normal and abnormal or emergency situations. To score 4 requires demonstrable evidence of effectiveness through impact on the environmental activities.

SCORE: LAST ASSESSMENT:

J

Q15: Are there established and maintained procedures for controlling all documentation required by BS7750?

4	Comprehensive document control procedures established and demonstrably effective.
3	Document control procedures in place.
2	Document control procedures established in some areas.
1	Document control procedures being developed.
0	No document control procedures exist.

Note: All aspects have to be in place to score highly. Having document control procedures is not enough. The procedures must ensure that documents have the proper identification, are periodically reviewed and revised and are available as current documents where they are required. To score 4 requires demonstrable evidence of effectiveness through impact on the environmental activities.

SCORE: LAST ASSESSMENT:

Q16: Are management responsibilities defined to ensure that control, verification, measurement and testing within the individual parts of the organisation are adequately co-ordinated and effectively performed?

4	Control responsibilities fully defined and co-ordinated demonstrably effective.
3	Control responsibilities defined in many parts of the organisation.
2	Control responsibilities partly defined.
1	Control responsibilities established in part but unco-ordinated.
0	Control responsibilities not defined.

Note: All aspects have to be in place to score highly. Management responsibilities must not only be defined, but also fully integrated across various departments and functions to meet the environmental objectives and targets. To score 4 requires demonstrable evidence of effectiveness through impact on the environmental activities.

SCORE: LAST ASSESSMENT:

Q17: Have the functions, activities and processes which have the potential to affect the environment and are relevant to the policy, objectives and targets, been identified and planned to ensure that they are carried out under controlled conditions?

4	Comprehensive and integrated controls over all identified areas.
3	Controls present in many identified areas.
2	Controls present in some areas.
1	Controls present in few areas, identification incomplete.
0	Identification and controls not present.

Note: All aspects have to be in place to score highly. Identification of the relevant areas must include all internal processes and also external activities, through procurement, transport, use and disposal. Work instructions should be designed to address all the relevant issues identified through the effects analysis, objectives and targets. To score 4 requires demonstrable evidence of effectiveness through impact on the environmental activities.

SCORE: LAST ASSESSMENT:

Q18: Are there established and maintained procedures for verification of compliance with specified requirements and the maintenance of relevant records?

4	Comprehensive verification procedures exist and demonstrably effective.
3	Verification procedures exist in many areas.
2	Verification procedures exist in some areas.
1	Verification procedures present in few areas.
0	Verification procedures not developed.

Note: All aspects have to be in place to score highly. Verification of compliance to specified requirements includes all the requirements from the programme, targets, manuals and works instructions, including direct and indirect effects. To score 4 requires demonstrable evidence of effectiveness through impact on the environmental activities.

SCORE: LAST ASSESSMENT:

Q19: Is the responsibility and authority for initiating investigation and corrective action in the event of non-compliance with specified requirements defined?

4	Corrective action responsibility and authority fully defined and demonstrably effective.
3	Corrective action responsibility and authority defined in many areas.
2	Corrective action responsibility and authority defined in some areas.
1	Corrective action responsibility and authority defined in few areas.
0	Corrective action responsibility and authority not defined.

Note: All aspects have to be in place to score highly. Corrective action responsibility and authority must be established and documented in the environmental manual or related documentation. To score 4 requires demonstrable evidence of effectiveness through impact on the environmental activities.

SCORE: LAST ASSESSMENT:

Q20: Are there established procedures for the investigation and corrective action in the event of non-compliance with specified requirements?

4	Corrective action procedures present in all key areas and demonstrably effective.
3	Corrective action procedures present in many areas.
2	Corrective action procedures present in some areas.
1	Corrective action procedures present in few areas.
0	Corrective action procedures not present.

Note: All aspects have to be in place to score highly. Corrective action procedures must allow determination of causes, action planning, initiate changes, control and change procedures to ensure effective resolution of the non-compliance. To score 4 requires demonstrable evidence of effectiveness through impact on the environmental activities.

SCORE: LAST ASSESSMENT:

Q21: Is there an established and maintained system of records to demonstrate compliance with the environmental management system requirements and the extent to which environmental objectives and targets have been met?

4	Comprehensive and accessible records available in all areas and demonstrably effective.
3	Records available in many areas.
2	Records available in some areas.
1	Records available in few areas.
0	Records not available.

Note: All aspects have to be in place to score highly. The records system will include procedures for appropriate management, be comprehensive across all key activity areas and provide an appropriate audit trail. To score 4 requires demonstrable evidence of effectiveness through impact on the environmental activities.

SCORE: LAST ASSESSMENT:

Q22: Are there established and maintained procedures for audits to be carried out to determine that environmental management activities conform to the programme and are effective in fulfilling the environmental policy?

4	Comprehensive EMS audits procedures present in all areas and demonstrably effective.
3	EMS audit procedures present in many areas.
2	EMS audit procedures present in some areas.
1	EMS audit procedures not fully developed.
0	EMS audit procedures do not exist.

Note: All aspects have to be in place to score highly. Having EMS audit procedures is not enough. They must be designed to determine that the management activities conform to the full environmental programme and are implemented as designed. They must look at the effectiveness of the EMS in achieving the policy objectives and targets. To score 4 requires demonstrable evidence of effectiveness through impact on the environmental activities.

SCORE: LAST ASSESSMENT:

Q23: Is there an established and maintained environmental management system audit plan?

4	Comprehensive audit plan exists in all areas and is demonstrably effective.
3	Audit plan exists in many areas.
2	Audit plan exists in some areas.
1	Audit plan exists in few areas.
0	There is not an established audit plan.

Note: All aspects have to be in place to score highly. Having an audit plan is not enough. It must identify the activities and areas, organisational structures, procedures, processes, documentation and performance to be assessed. The frequency, and ownership must be defined. The independence of the audit staff, expertise, resources and protocol must be defined. To score 4 requires demonstrable evidence of effectiveness through impact on the environmental activities.

SCORE: LAST ASSESSMENT:

Q24: Are there established procedures for reporting the results of environmental management systems audits to those responsible for the activity or area audited?

4	Comprehensive audit reporting procedures exist in all areas and are demonstrably effective.
3	Audit reporting procedures exist in many areas.
2	Audit reporting procedures exist in some areas.
1	Audit reporting procedures exist in few areas.
0	Audit reporting procedures do not exist.

Note: All aspects have to be in place to score highly. Having audit reporting procedures is not enough. They must address the non-conformity areas, the effectiveness in achieving objectives and targets, the effectiveness of corrective action from previous audits, formal recommendations and (if required) procedure for the publication of findings. To score 4 requires demonstrable evidence of effectiveness through impact on the environmental activities.

SCORE: LAST ASSESSMENT:

Q25: Have the organisation's management reviewed the environmental management system adopted to ensure its continuing suitability and effectiveness?

4	Comprehensive management reviews completed and demonstrably effective.
3	Management reviews take place in many areas.
2	Management reviews take place in some areas.
1	Management reviews are not fully developed.
0	Management reviews do not exist.

Note: All aspects have to be in place to score highly. It is not enough to have management reviews. They must comprehensively look at all aspects of the existing system including audit results. They should consider wider implications of changes in legislation, organisation, roles and responsibilities as well as environmental performance objectives and targets. To score 4 requires demonstrable evidence of effectiveness through impact on the environmental activities.

SCORE: LAST ASSESSMENT:

SUMMARY OF RESPONSES:	DEPARTMENT/FUNCTION:
Question and subject	Response
1. Initial review	
2. Environmental management system	
3. Environmental policy	
4. Responsibility and authority	
5. Verification resources and personnel	
6. Management representative	
7. Communication procedures	
8. Training needs	
9. Register of requirements	
10 Communications	
11 Environmental effects register	
12 Environmental objectives and targets	
13 Environmental programme	
14 Environmental management manual	
15 Documentation control	
16 Management responsibility for controls	
17 Controlled conditions	
18 Verification of compliance	
19 Responsibility for non-compliance	
20 Procedures for non-compliance resolution	
21 Environmental management records	
22 EMS audit procedures	
23 EMS audit plan	
24 EMS audit reporting	
25 Environmental management reviews	
Total	

Completed by: Date:

22

External assessment

One of the requirements for the design of BS7750: a specification for environmental management systems was the need for a standard against which compliance could be assessed and certified by an independent body. The success of the committee in designing such a standard can be seen by the pressure to develop assessment and certification schemes from those companies in the pilot programme.

It's your business

What does certification of compliance mean for those wishing to attain BS7750 registration?

It may be useful to view BS7750 as a benchmark or yardstick against which the EMS you have installed can be assessed. The benchmark sets out the elements of the system to be in place *inside* your organisation. The first specification clause requires you to document *your* system and then ensure it is effective in operation. Fig 22.1 illustrates the relationship.

You know your business, the system must be integrated into your business, so it must become *your* system. BS7750 is the benchmark for assessment and review internally and subsequently externally by an appropriately skilled assessor.

The development of third party certification is not a straightforward matter for a new standard in an area like environmental management.

Certification progress

One of the objectives of the pilot programme is to assess the feasibility of certification and the skills, systems and protocols appropriate for such certification.

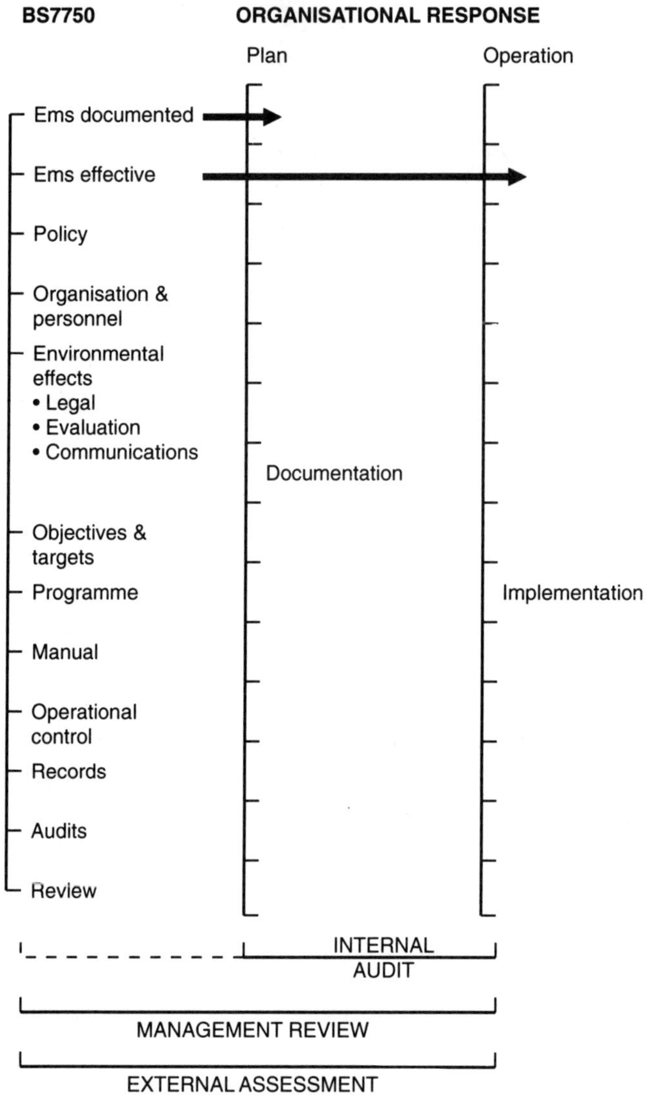

Fig. 22.1 BS7750 requirements and your business

Members of the Association of British Certification Bodies (ABCB) are supporting the pilot programme to provide advice and guidance on the certification issues. ABCB members offer third party certification against standards and specifications, from BS5750 quality systems to product specifications.

BS7750 is currently under review in the light of experience from the pilot programme and the revisions to the proposed Eco-Management and audit regulation, referred to in the foreword and annex C; as the regulation has changed, some revision is certain.

Establishing an assessment practice and protocol against a new management system standard, likely to change in 1993–4 has led most certification bodies to hold back from offering certification at this time.

THE ACCREDITATION ISSUE

A further factor influencing the offering of third party certification is the availability of accreditation. Accreditation in the UK is provided by the National Accreditation Council for Certification Bodies (NACCB). At this time, the NACCB does not have a mandate to accredit bodies certifying for compliance to BS7750. Any action to do this will be linked to the need for accreditation of verifiers under the proposed eco-management and audit regulation. Until the accreditation agency for the proposed regulation verification is agreed, it is also deemed premature for certification bodies to offer un-accredited certification to industry.

Meanwhile a great deal of useful work is taking place to establish the appropriate practices, protocols and skill requirements through the pilot programme. So that when the time is right, accredited certification will be available, probably in 1994, appropriately linked to verification against the eco-management and audit regulation requirements.

The certification issues

As a result of the ABCB members' work in the pilot programme, some issues have been discussed.

WHAT DOES THE ASSESSMENT BODY CERTIFICATE INDICATE WHEN APPLIED TO AN EMS?

In BS5750, certification confirms a supplier's quality management system meets a standard, to deliver a specified product or service that is defined and documented in a contract between two parties.

In BS7750, the environmental management system is being assessed to a standard, to deliver a specified environmental performance set by the organisation as a result of policy and an analysis of his environmental effects and legal requirements. Therefore the assessor will need to understand both the EMS and the environmental performance to confirm compliance.

Yet the environmental performance is in a direct relationship to the policy, directives and targets of the organisation. Is it expected that the certification body acts as arbiter to those elements of the system? Most certification bodies would say no, that it is the role of industry and legislation to define the levels of performance required. The certification body can provide assurance that systems are in place to BS7750 and that the environmental performance meets the policy, objectives and targets.

There is a role here for the industry sector codes of practice to establish appropriate models of policy, objectives and targets to provide guidance to the organisation and certification bodies.

WHAT EXPERTISE IS NEEDED?

In addition to quality system assessment skills, it is clear that industry knowledge and environmental performance knowledge will be required in carrying out assessments to BS7750. Industry knowledge, for familiarity with the issues and special processes involved; environmental performance knowledge to ensure that test, measurement methods and other practices are appropriate.

These mixed skills may be present in individuals, but it is more likely that a team will provide an appropriate mix. Industry will also require the assessment team to be a flexible part of a BS5750 assessment programme, so these skills are also needed.

HOW WILL EXTERNAL PARTIES VIEW CERTIFICATION?

What will be the perceived view of the value of certification to BS7750 by outside organisations and individuals?

Will HMIP or local authority inspectors view the certificate as providing evidence of legal compliance? Will BS7750 be deemed a Best Available Technique? Will the pressure groups and public regard the certificate as a valuable confirmation of commitment or as a 'rubber stamp' that adds little value to the environmental debate?

The signs currently are that all external parties regard the development of BS7750 as a positive contribution to improving and benchmarking the environmental management status of organisations. It is recognised that it does not imply perfection, but that it is a significant step along the road to continual improvement of environmental performance.

BS7750 and the proposed Eco-Management and audit Regulation

Appendices 1 and 2 cover a more detailed analysis of the current requirements of these documents. A high degree of compatibility exists as you would expect from the parallel developments, designed to complement one another. One significant difference remains between the two, and that is the public statement requirement in the proposed regulation, not required by BS7750, unless referred to in the policy, objectives and targets.

More and more companies now recognise the value of open declarations of environmental performance – from Norsk Hydro, Dow, ICI and others, it is an essential part of establishing credibility in the eyes of the community. If you are not willing to publish your performance, the logic is that you have something to hide.

The final form of the regulation uses significant portions of BS7750 as the EMS requirement. We can look forward to a future where assessed capability to BS7750, together with relevant public statements provides the appropriate confirmation of compliance with the proposed regulation scheme requirements.

Conclusion

In establishing an effective environmental management system in your organisation, you have prepared the ground for future third party certification. When these services are available, you will be able to guide the management team through that achievement with confidence.

At the start of the book, I indicated that the process of establishing an EMS is a change management process. As a result of the implementation of the programme, your organisation has changed, but it does not stop here. Implicit in the management system is the continual review of the system, of your environmental performance and of trends in requirements from legislation to community issues. By continually responding to these changing needs, and by involving everyone, everywhere in the organisation in contributing to improving environmental performance, we are all a step nearer to attaining our overall goal of sustainable development.

Appendix I

BS7750: Specification for environmental management systems

Introduction

Work on BS7750 commenced in 1991 with the formation of a technical committee at the British Standards Institution (BSI). The committee consisted of over 40 members from many parts of industry, commerce, government and legislative bodies as well as interested associations and institutes. Their combined expertise in environmental management systems was pooled to develop a new British Standard. Publication of the draft in June 1991 for the public consultation phase proved to be a significant event. Outselling all previous drafts for comment, it attracted significant public comment and was even published as a draft in two other countries. Since then, there have been many articles and speeches on the subject and many conferences. It has changed the vocabulary of the environmental community and introduced a fresh focus for environmental problem-solving – from environmental auditing to environmental management, from 'downstream' problem identification and fixing, to 'upstream' problem prediction and management.

A pilot programme to test the Standard has grown from a plan to involve 40 companies, when first considered, to an exercise that currently involves nearly 200 implementing organisations supported by over 30 trade associations and other interest groups. Altogether nearly 400 separate organisations are participating in 35 working groups. In addition to testing the Standard in use, they are considering the need for related industry guides and looking at the implications of third-party assessment and certification. There is also activity on similar standards at European and international levels.

The brief

The brief to the technical committee included the following:

The new Standard should be

1. related to BS5750 to ensure that the new standard would meet the requirements of a quality system, and also meet the needs of those companies that had used BS5750 as a model for the quality system for their products or services.
2. While being compatible with BS5750, the new standard should be separate, both to ensure that the management's focus on environmental performance of the organisation is paramount and to provide a separate yardstick for assessment of environmental performance. Not all organisations use BS5750 for their products and services and it should not be a prerequisite to attaining an appropriate environmental system performance assessment.

3. The new Standard should be generic. It should be written in such a way that it provides guidance for companies large and small, and whether in manufacturing, service or other sectors.
4. The new Standard should be holistic. It should encourage a comprehensive look at the organisation including all aspects of a company's activities and the life-cycle effects of the product or service provided to ensure that the resulting environmental programmes are relevant to the issues it faces.
5. The new Standard should be assessable. It should be capable of being used as an assessment tool that encourages compliance certification and, if required, registration.

The contents

To meet the brief, BS7750 is laid out in the form of a single easy-to-read and self-contained document for managers in organisations of any size. It is numbered in a way that reflects the linkage to BS5750: Quality systems. Internally it is laid out in the form of:

- A foreword
- The specification including:
  - introduction
  - scope
  - informative references
  - definitions
  - environmental management system requirements

- Annexes:
  - A: guide to environmental management system requirements
  - B: links to BS5750: Quality systems
  - C: links to draft EC eco-audit regulation
  - D: bibliography of glossaries

FOREWORD

The foreword positions the Standard in relation to other documentation, sector guides, BS5750 and the draft Eco-audit Regulation, as well as introducing the concept of integrated compliance assessment. It also specifies the planned review to be undertaken in the light of experience from the pilot programme and the final version of the proposed eco-audit regulation planned for publication early in 1993. The Foreword indicates the parallel approach to quality system requirement, assessment and accreditation assumed within the Standard.

THE SPECIFICATION

The specification begins with an **Introduction** which relates the Standard to increasingly stringent environmental legislation, environmental audit activities and the need for these to be carried out within the framework of a structured environmental management system.

Figure A1.1 (which is based on Figure 1 of the Standard's introduction) provides an elemental approach to achieving the standard requirements, although this is not a prescribed route. The Introduction reinforces the links to BS5750 and the draft EC Eco-audit Regulation requirement for an 'internal environmental protection system'.

Clause 1, Scope describes the intent, objective or intended use of the contents. The scope clause is intended to establish how and where the Standard might be used. The clause states that the Standard can be used by any organisation. An organisation is defined as any organised body: it might be a multinational corporation or a small High Street business. The standard is applicable for any organisation that wishes to assure itself of compliance with a stated environmental policy and demonstrate that compliance to others. This last point is key to the 'specification' approach, the use of 'shall' in clause 4, which allows an independent assessment programme to be effectively carried out and certification to be gained.

Clause 2 provides a note on **informative references** to other Standards which are listed inside the back cover. These include BS5750: Quality system and BS7229: Quality system auditing.

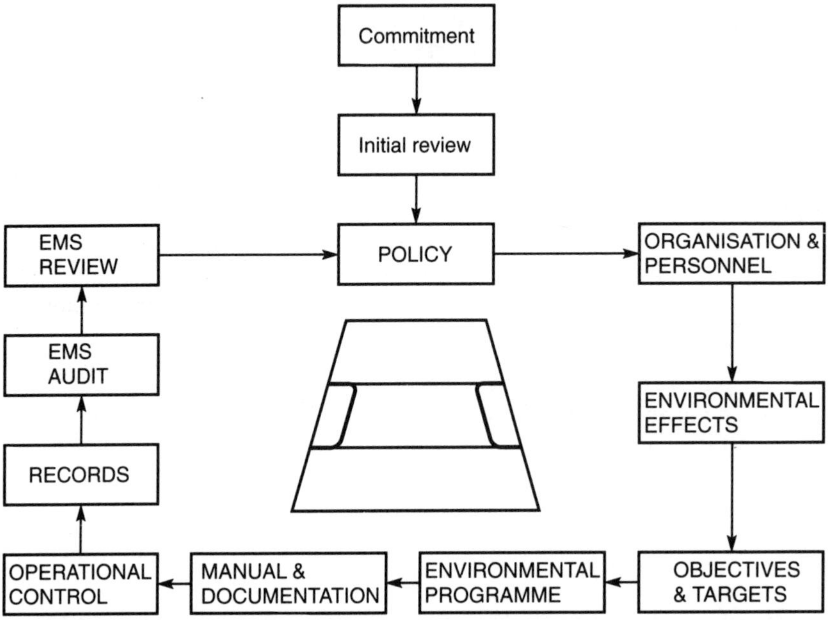

Fig. A1.1 Schematic diagram of the elements in the implementation of an environmental management system

Clause 3, Definitions, covers the key words or phrases that have particular meaning in the document. This is to ensure that there is clarity in the use of words within the Standard.

(Notable by its absence, is the phrase 'environmental audit' which is used to describe different types of systematic assessment of environmental performance – due diligence for acquisitions, life-cycle assessments of products, site audits, audits against legislative compliance, etc. Forms of systematic assessments of environmental performance include:

(a) A preparatory review which provides a baseline for developing the environmental management system. See Annex A.1.2.

(b) An environmental effects evaluation which evaluates the significance of the environmental effects of the activities of the organisation. This includes products and services, both current and proposed.

(c) An environmental management audit which establishes the compliance of the system with the specified requirements.

(d) An environmental management review which establishes the overall performance of the system, including audits, with a view to system changes and improvements to policy objectives and targets.)

Clause 4 details the **environmental management system requirements.**

1. A written system must be established and maintained in the organisation to implement the environmental policy, objectives and targets. The written processes then have to be implemented effectively.
2. A written policy statement that is relevant to the organisation's activities must be communicated internally and externally. It must be related to the objectives and targets and commit the organisation to continual environmental performance improvement.
3. A description of organisational responsibilities and authority, and verification resources must be documented. Including the management representative EMS and the personnel who are trained to support the programme.
4. A set of procedures to record relevant regulatory requirements, significant environmental effects and communications with interested parties must be established.
5. A set of procedures to establish quantified objectives and targets throughout the organisation, relevant to other business goals, must exist.
6. A programme to achieve the documented objectives must be established.
7. An environmental management manual to co-ordinate the relevant documentation must be produced. Documents must be managed and controlled, current and effective.
8. Control measurement, testing and verification procedures must be established to ensure that the processes meet requirements and that where failure is detected, appropriate action is initiated to correct problems.
9. A records system must be established to ensure that adequate information exists to demonstrate compliance with the environmental management system, objectives and targets.
10. Environmental management audit plans, procedures and protocols must be used to assess and report system status.
11. Review of the environmental management system, including the result of system audits, must be made, to ensure the arrangements are appropriate and effective.

The layout of the Standard is designed to show the approach as a logical process, shown sequentially. Inevitably such a process is not unidirectional. There will be jumps forward and steps repeated in the light of improved knowledge.

THE ANNEXES

Annex A, provides guidance to the requirement statements in clause 4 but does not add to or remove any requirements, i.e. it is informative.

Clause A.1.1 indicates that the system application assumes a pro-active approach, integrated into an organisation's day-to-day management system. There are close links with occupational health and safety, particularly in activities where the product has potentially high risks, e.g. chemicals or petroleum. (It is interesting that the organisations which scored highest in the self-assessment questionnaire attached to the BSI pilot programme for BS7750 were in the chemical and petrochemical industries.) However, the system is not designed to address health and safety management issues.

The clause on preparatory environmental review (A.1.2) has no direct link to the requirements clause because, although it is a recommended activity to initiate action on developing an EMS, it is not part of an ongoing environmental management system.

Clause A.2 provides guidance on policy ownership and range of content, from waste minimisation to strategic planning issues. Continual, step-by-step (rather than continuous) improvement is stressed.

Organisation and personnel guidance is given in clause (A.3), focusing on the role of management representatives and their relationship with the managers. Training and motivational aspects of the EMS are discussed.

In considering the environmental effects requirements (A.4), the guide focuses on the wide scope of the effects analysis. It encourages a broad look at the organisation, the suppliers to that organisation, past and planned activities, and normal and abnormal operating conditions.

Considering the whole organisation (see Fig. A1.2) is implicit in the guidance and specification. Also implicit is the need to assess the cradle-to-grave aspects of products. Sometimes called life-cycle analysis (see Fig. A1.3), this is another form of environmental audit which focuses on the environmental effects of a particular product.

Clause A.5, environmental objectives and targets, reinforce the quantifiable and accountable aspects of environmental performance improvement. The reference to continual improvement over a time frame supports the concept of a progressive, continuing step-by-step improvement.

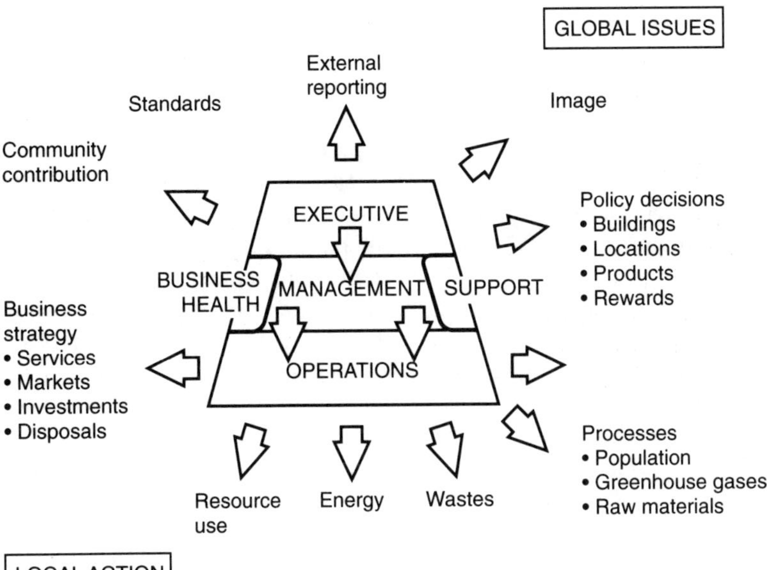

All organisations have environmental effects from all elements of internal activity

Fig. A1.2 Environmental effects from *all* aspects of a whole organisation's internal activity

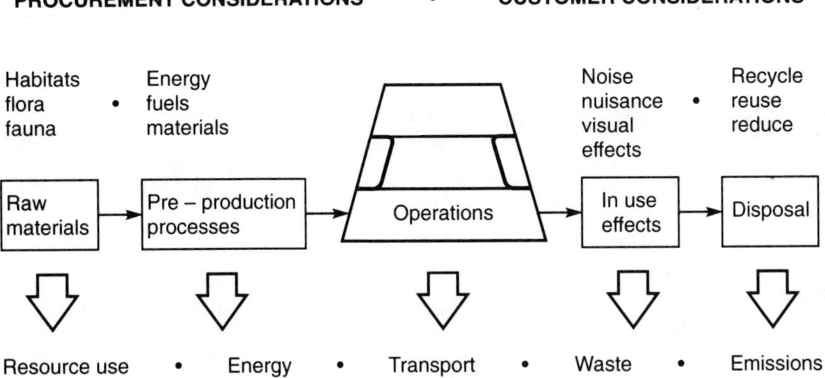

Fig. A1.3 Environmental effects of a product's life-cycle

Guidance on the programme to be followed is given in clause A.6. It supports the need for a comprehensive roadmap of how the organisation will achieve its objectives and targets, including past activities, current processes, future plans and the upstream/downstream effects.

Guidance on the environmental management manual and other documentation is offered in clause A.7. It supports the two aspects of the specification: (a) the scope of the documentation, indicating that it may be a 'signpost document, and not an encyclopaedic reference book; and (b) that all relevant documentation should be appropriately controlled.

Clause A.8, operational control, indicates the extent to which procedures should be established to deal with all the implementation of the environmental programme in the relevant parts of the business. Verification includes statistically valid measurement processes and calibration procedures. Appropriate corrective action plans include investigation and changes to address shortfalls in compliance.

Records (A.9) should be appropriate to demonstrate the effectiveness of the system and system compliance. This includes accident and incident data.

Clause A.10 clarifies that audits of the management system may be carried out by external consultants or internal staff, providing they are independent of the area being audited.

A.11 provides guidance on the extent of the management review.

Annex B demonstrates the links between BS7750 and BS5750, EN29000 and ISO9000. It supports the development of an EMS within organisations that have used the quality systems standard as a model.

Annex C demonstrates the links between BS7750 and the EC Eco-audit Regulation, which (at the time of writing) is a draft regulation published in January 1992. One of the objectives of S7750 is to provide a model for the EMS element of the regulation requirements. A table is included in Annex C which provides a visible link to the regulation requirements.

Annex D provides a bibliography of the reference material.

Appendix II

EC Eco-Management and audit Regulation

Introduction

The proposed EC Eco-Management and audit Regulation, is formally entitled: 'Proposal for a Council Regulation (EEC) allowing voluntary participation by companies in the industrial sector in a Community Eco-management and audit scheme'.

The last publicly available version was the edition published in the *Official Journal of the European Commission* in December 1992. The version reviewed here is the revised draft issued in December 1993, and represents the current thinking, reflecting the move away from eco-auditing to an eco-management and auditing scheme. Because of the continuing developing nature of the Regulation, check the final version, due for publication in June 1993.

> NOTE: A Regulation is a powerful legislative tool within the EC. Providing legislation that, when adopted, automatically becomes law in all member states.
>
> This is different from a Directive, that requires legislative interpretation by Member States own parliaments e.g.: The EC directive on environmental assessment.

This regulation was planned as part of the Fifth Environmental Action Programme. It supports the principles of the polluter pays and the public availability of environmental information, particularly from industry.

As a Regulation, and if adopted by the EC it will automatically become UK law, this document requires Members states to participate in the setting-up of a *voluntary* European wide Eco-Management and auditing scheme, focused on certain industrial sectors.

The reward for participation in the scheme is the use of a statement of participation. This statement mark can be used with environmental statements, on brochures and documents, on letter heading and advertising material, but not on products. It must always be used in conjunction with the name of the site to which it relates.

To earn the right to display the statement of participation, participating companies must:

- Adopt a company environmental policy.
- Conduct an environmental review of the site identified by the company.
- Introduce as a result of the review, an environmental programme and management system.
- Carry out environmental audits of the site.
- In the light of the findings of the audit, revise the programme and set objectives for continuous improvement.
- Prepare an environmental statement specific to the site.
- Have the environmental policy, programme, management system, review or audit procedure and statement examined to verify they meet the requirements of the regulation.
- Forward the validated environmental statement to the competent body of the relevant member state.

ELEMENT OF THE REGULATION

The Regulation has the following elements:

Articles 1–20 specifying the main requirement and operating clauses of the regulation.

Annex I which is in four parts concerning environmental policies, programmes and management systems.

A: Environmental policies, objectives and programmes.
B: Environmental management systems.
C: Issues to be covered.
D: Good management practices.

Annex II which states the requirements concerning environmental auditing.

A: Objectives.
B: Scope.
C: Organisation and resources.
D: Planning and preparation for site audit.
E: Audit activities.
F: Reporting audit findings and conclusions.

G: Audit follow-up.
H: Audit frequency.

Annex III which states the requirements concerning the accreditation of environmental verifiers and the function of the verifier.

A: Requirements for the accreditation of Environmental Verifiers.
B: The function of the verifiers.

Annex IV which indicates model statements of participation in the scheme.

Annex V which indicates the information to be provided to the competent bodies at the time of application for registration or submission or a subsequent validated environmental statement.

What is in the elements

The introductory statement present in early versions has been ommitted in the latest draft. When published in December 1992 the statement covered:

- The EEC articles of the Treaty of Rome, European Parliament and European Commission.
- The EEC environmental policy and fifth environmental action programme.
- Focus on polluter pays principle and pollution elimination at source.
- Recognises the increasing complexity of environmental protection system.
- Recognises the value of systematic environmental auditing to companies.
- Recognises the value of public information about companies environmental performance.
- Recognises the need for standardisation in certification of internal environmental management systems.
- Recognises the benefits of a voluntary scheme.
- Recognises the need for independent validation of the public statements, by accredited verifiers.
- Accepts the requirement to review the regulation in the light of experience gained.

THE ARTICLES

The main Articles which define the regulation requirements cover the following:

Article 1: Defines the objectives of the scheme, allows voluntary participation by companies in a scheme to promote continuous improvement in environmental performance. This is planned to be done through encouraging participating companies to establish environmental policies, programmes and management systems related to specific sites. Then to carry out systematic, objective and periodic evaluation of the performance of the such elements and to provide information to the public about the site environmental performance.

Article 2: A series of definitions of key words and phrases, from 'environmental policy' to 'competent body'. It includes reference to the industrial activities covered by the scheme.

Article 3: Explains the requirements for companies participating in the scheme. From adopting a policy to forwarding the validated statement specific to each site audited. It ties in the relevant Annexes where appropriate to clarify the requirements.

Article 4: Covers the auditing and validation requirements, including the status of internal auditors, audit frequency, and the accredited environmental verifiers independence. It further identifies the scope of the verification activities and the confidentiality of the verifiers activities.

Article 5: Defines the requirements for the environmental statement. When it should be prepared, its style and contents. It clarifies the need for subsequent, simplified statements and the reduced requirement for small and medium sized enterprises.

Article 6: States the requirement for accreditation of the environmental verifiers and the responsibilities of Member States in establishing the accreditation systems for verifiers.

Article 7: Requires the maintenance of a list of accredited verifiers to be available in the UK and EC, to be published annually in the *Official Journal of the European Communities*.

Article 8: Requires the maintenance of a register of participating sites by the competent body, and information on the addition and deletion of sites to the register.

Article 9: Refers to the collation of lists from Member States to the commission, who will publish these in the *Official Journal of the European Communities*.

Article 10: Defines the statements of participation that may be used in conjunction with the logo.

Article 11: Indicates that fees may be required by Member States to support the administration of the scheme and accreditation of environmental verifiers.

Article 12: Indicates the relationship between the requirements of the Regulation and National, European and International Standards, and certification. Providing the standards and procedures are recognised by the commission, and the certification carried out by appropriately accredited bodies, will be deemed as meeting the requirements of the regulation.

Article 13: Indicates the encouragement to Member States to take a pro-active approach to supporting small and medium-sized enterprises in the scheme, by providing technical assistance.

Article 14: This clause indicates the encouragement to apply the provisions of the Scheme to sectors other than those defined, e.g. Service organisations.

Article 15: Requires Member States to inform companies and the public of the scheme.

Article 15a: Requires Member States to take appropriate legal action in cases of non-compliance with the regulation.

Article 16: Requires the Commission to adapt the Annexes in the light of experience, linked to the work of the Committee referred to in Article 18.

Article 17: Requires the setting-up by Member States of independent, neutral Competent Bodies responsible for implementing the Regulation.

Article 18: Establishes the role of a Committee, chaired by the Commission, which will be responsible for commenting on the proposed measures to be taken through a weighted voting procedure.

Article 19: Requires the Commission to review the scheme in the light of the experience gained during its operation into more than 5 years after entry into force.

Article 20: Establishes that entry into force of the Regulation is designated as 1 January 1993 and that it shall apply with effect from 1 October 1994.

THE ANNEXES

Annex I: Part A: Describes the requirements for environmental policy setting, objectives and programmes.

The documented policy and programme have to be linked to those of the company as a whole. Adopted and reviewed at the highest level, and publicly available. As well as a legal compliance, the policy shall commit the organisation to continual improvement of environmental performance.

From the policy shall be developed, quantified objectives and targets at all relevant levels in the company.

The company must establish an environmental programme to implement the objectives, at each relevant level and in relation to key activities.

Part B: Addresses the environmental management system requirements and looks at the need for policy, objectives and targets, organisation and responsibility allocation, and environmental effects evaluation and register procedure, including regulatory matters. A section on operational control and monitoring, including non-compliance and corrective action procedures. Environmental documentation records and environmental audits.

(All of this material has a basis in BS7750, with some of the text directly quoted, other parts slightly adapted.)

Part C: Describes the issues to be covered in the environmental management system: Including the reduction of environmental impact, energy management, raw materials management, waste avoidance, planning and production processes. The environmental performance of suppliers and contractors, accidents and emergency planning, staff training and communications are all covered.

Part D: Describes a set of good management practices and principles of action. These include a sense of environmental responsibility at all levels in the organisation, assessing the environmental impact of activities regularly, measures taken to reduce or eliminate pollution, regular monitoring programmes and emergency action procedures. These will include co-operation with public authorities, an open dialogue with the public on environmental activities, information to customers and the management of contractors.

Annex II: Describes the requirements concerning environmental auditing based on the application of ISO10011:1990 Auditing Quality Systems. The references in the text interpret the standards to apply to environmental auditing by referring to the following:

'Quality system' = 'Environmental management system'
'Quality standards' = 'Environmental standard'
'Quality audit' = 'Environmental audit'.

This is intended to allow quality system audit protocols and procedures to be used for the assessment of the environmental management system. The annex goes on to describe key parts of the audit procedure:

A: Defining the objectives and frequency of the audit, which must include assessment of the management systems, policy, programme and regulatory compliance.
B: Requires the scope to be defined, including the subject areas, the activities, the environmental standards and period of time to be considered.
C: Establishes the knowledge base required of auditors and the requirement for top company management to support the audit activity with appropriate independent resources.
D: Requires that the audit plan balances the resources, roles and responsibilities of the participants in the audit. Including a familiarisation and a review of the conclusions of previous audits.
E: Describes in detail the audit activities, including site discussions, inspections and reviews. The steps are defined as: understanding the system; assessing the strengths and weaknesses; gathering evidence; evaluating the findings; preparing the conclusions and final reporting.
F: Describes in more detail the requirements for the reporting of the audit findings and conclusions in written form to the senior management. The report should include the scope; information on the state of compliance with policy; information on the effectiveness of monitoring and demonstrate the need for corrective action where required.
G: Requires the preparation of a plan of action to implement the corrective action defined.
H: Defines the guidance for audit frequency. This must not be at intervals greater than three years. The actual frequency being decided by top management, related to the nature of the activities on the site; the emissions, wastes, energy consumption etc., the significance of the issues discovered and the history of the problems.

Annex III: Is concerned with the accreditation of environmental verifiers and the function of the verifier.

A: Defines the requirements for the accreditation of environmental verifiers, including competence, independence and objectivity, the procedures and organisation structures.

It refers to the accreditation of individuals as well as organisations.

In defining the accreditation process the text assumes the existence of accreditation bodies who will assess the proposed verifier against predetermined criteria and for specific areas of scope.

It requires the continuing supervision of accredited environmental verifiers at regular intervals not exceeding three years.

B: Defines the function of the verifier, in assessing the all aspects of the environmental policy, programme, systems, audit and statements. It includes a review compliance with the requirements of the regulation itself. All the work of the verifier to be done under a written agreement and will conclude with a verifier's report which will define the degree of compliance observed.

Index

■